ROCK BOTTOM

ROCK BOTTOM

A MULTI-GENRE ANTHOLOGY

IVY GRAVES WILLOW LEWIS
GINGER MOONWITCH A. TWISTED
MARNEY CARROLL VIVIAN RAGE L. V. ELDRIDGE
L. LESTRANGE TIM GRAYSON M. T. SOMMER
BELLADONNA B.A. MCCLUSKEY SCARLETT INK
LLIANNE OLIVO SYLAS SEABROOK C. J. JENKINS
ALANA DAIL DEANN SOLEIL LEE ADAM
K.M. AVERY K. D. LAVENDER S. B. STRICKLAND
KC RENZEL A. DOUBLE PASTEL WREN

KC RENZEL

A. DOUBLE

PASTEL WREN

COVER DESIGN: IVY GRAVES / CANVA STOCK

INTERIOR FORMATTING: IVY GRAVES / CANVA STOCK

CONSENT MATTERS

Risk-Aware Consensual Kink (RACK) and Enlightened Consent are two current approaches for BDSM. However, the framework and language are always evolving. Please research your local legislation and peer reviewed articles on the subject.

Having capacity and ability, being explicit in communication, giving and getting permission. It is ongoing and retractable at any moment.

Safewords, the traffic light system, and other nonverbal signals are examples of communication.

ACKNOWLEDGMENT OF COUNTRY

The authors acknowledge and pay their respects to the Traditional Owners of the land on which they live and write.

They pay their respects to Country and Creatures.

They extend her respect to all First Nations people and acknowledge Elders past and present.

ALWAYS WAS, ALWAYS WILL BE.

For those at rock bottom, whatever that looks like for you.

YOU MATTER

Have you ever felt so alone that even the voices in your head told you to give up?

Yet, you're still here.

Maybe it was the friend who called at the right time, or the face of your dog that kept you breathing.

Edited by Ivy Graves and Willow Lewis, this multi-author, multi-genre anthology is a safe space for the unseen, outcasts and black sheep.

Raw emotion from the trenches.

These stories represent the silent struggle, giving a voice to those who fight in the dark.

You are not alone. Rock bottom isn't the end. It is often the point at which you start to craft who you want to be, from the ashes. We see you.

You matter.

You are not alone in the darkness.

WARNING

These works have been left in the raw form submitted by the authors. They all contain potentially triggering themes. We have attempted to put a trigger warning before each piece. Some poems were left open to interpretation.

Please look after your mental health, and take your time reading these stories.

Many were painfully healing to write, but in doing so, many triggers were brought up. We have decided to leave the words exactly as they fell, so we hope that you, dear reader, can feel just a sliver of the emotions the writer felt as they shared them with you.

May they heal you in some way.

Thank you for supporting us.

Sometimes it feels like no one wants to listen and no one cares.

Together we rise.

Together we heal.

1
BETTER WITHOUT ME
ONE MOM'S STRUGGLE WITH POSTPARTUM PSYCHOSIS

WILLOW LEWIS

Post-partum psychosis, Self-harm / Cutting, Depression, Suicide attempt, Mental institutionalizations

Authors note:

Birth, either in the traditional sense, with or without pain medication, or by C-section, can be beautiful. This is for moms who struggle with postpartum depression and postpartum psychosis. The ones who struggle to find the will to live, and the moms who do everything in their power to keep it together while holding the weight of the world on their shoulders. You're not alone! You're seen, heard, and loved. Sometimes moms don't have a village; we ARE the village.

CHRISTMAS LOOMS over my head like a beacon of death. Laughter paired with pitter-patters of little feet can be heard throughout our home. I sit there having many thoughts. "They would be better off without me. My husband will remarry. They don't need a broken mom."

A mom who fantasizes about taking her life. Air never fills my lungs. This broken woman is supposed to be caring for 8 little hearts. Hearts that know little of death. Yet all I feel is sadness. Their laughter should put this heart back together.

7 little souls sleep peacefully in their little beds—stuffed animals littering their beds. Little coos come from our 8th little soul who's sleeping in my arms. Turning to the love of my life, I say, "Remind our kids that I love them. I love you!"

Handing our newborn to my husband, I sneak into the bathroom where the bottle of relief is waiting for me. Beckoning me like a saviour. Relinquishing my little family from having to be stuck with a broken, damaged person who only burdens them with demons they never created.

Bang. Bang. Bang.

"What are you doing? Open the door, babe!" I

lie through my teeth as I keep my voice strong, "I'm just going potty". A lie he knows I'm telling. The door busts open, his shocked face now looking at the open bottle in my hands, yanking it out of my grasp. He pulls me into a hug, asking me questions he knows won't be the truth.

These thoughts aren't my own. Yet my mind screams at how worthless I am, how anyone could do a better job than I ever could. Thoughts scream at me day and night. There's no controlling them, arguing with them, or wishing them away.

Holding me during the night, even though I say I'm fine, yet he never believes the lie. Why is he fighting for me when all I'm trying to do is release them and myself from this hell?

Brad was bound and determined to save me, even when all I wanted was for him to let me go. He kept watch, my own personal angel, refusing to let his wife fade even more than she already had. Whispered words grazed past my ear as my husband said, "They needed me."

Nothing he said made an impact on this heart.

Doesn't he realize the storm that's raging in my head?

The broken, shattered version of a failure. Failure of not swallowing that bottle of meds. Failure of not releasing my family from the burden of myself.

My visions of my family having a better life with a better mom, a better wife, a happy woman. That woman would read them bedtime stories and never raise her voice.

A mom whom people loved. A loving wife who was submissive, who could handle all of life's problems with grace. I took ending my life as the answer to my suffering, their suffering. No longer would they have to live a life with a mom who's beyond perfect. Between the crying and pleading for my husband to let me go back to the bathroom to finish the job, my eyes had finally closed for a few hours of sleep.

My options: the one and only OBGYN clinic was sold, no more postpartum care, no one to fix the brokenness inside me. The closest OBGYN clinic was an hour away, with a waiting list a mile long. My only option was going to the walk-in clinic in the next town over.

Stepping out of my Explorer, I round the door to grab the baby carrier with my newborn. All those phone calls to family and friends that went unanswered. All the "You wanted kids, so you raise them."

I didn't need help to raise my children. I wanted to sleep; I wanted a hot shower; I wanted to feel something, anything.

Stepping up to the counter, I bravely stated I needed to see a Dr, right now. "We have a waiting list. We can get you in 2 weeks. What day works? "You don't understand, I need to see someone now". Shuffling me into a small room, Dr. comes in asking the typical questions. "Are you ok with your baby? Do you need us to take her?" Tears are streaming down my face as I reply, "No, don't touch her".

Do they not understand? I wanted to kill myself, not hurt my child. Thinking about someone touching my daughter has my blood boiling. She is mine! They couldn't take her from me! Someone called my husband; he showed up with concern etched on his face. The lines that ran deep from worry and lack of sleep. Forehead kisses, hugs, and I love you's were said before he takes our daughter with him. Nurses sit outside my door, expecting me to lose it. Hustle and bustle continue in the hallways, but I pay no attention. Looking around at all the locked cabinets, nothing within arm's reach. I don't want to do this anymore.

This is just the waiting game until transportation carries me away to the psych ward.

The car ride is silent besides the two drivers making small chat here and there amongst themselves. Hours later, the transportation team is walking me into the psych hospital.

Every possession has been taken, just the night gown that has been covering my ass. Nurses have given me cleaning products, as I don't recall when my last shower was. I know my baby spit up, titty sweat, and postpartum vagina discharge leaking is a smell that needs to swirl down the drain. Hot water droplets wash away all the dried-up tears.

Voices fill the hall, hall monitoring checks; meds are being handed out. Patients are roaming around with emotionless stares; some patients refuse to come out of their rooms unless it's for a work class, counselling appointment, or food.

Tears come, and the guilt eats at me every passing minute. Anti-depressants aren't making me feel better. It's the same thing on repeat. Far from a vacation – living in my brain is a fucking nightmare. Therapy, group therapy, and psychiatrist appointments come and go in a blur.

One week has passed before I'm discharged. Medication has made everyday numbness almost bearable. I've passed my psychological screening; they think I'm safe, safe from myself. Yet these thoughts keep coming, not as strongly, yet they linger.

Laughing at the appropriate times, tears that come and go. The scariest part is when it's "lights out". Every sound has me on edge.

Every shadow is a figment of my imagination. A crying baby wakes me from a fretful night's sleep. I'm not home in our bed with our newborn cradled in my arms.

I'm lying on this cold hospital bed with the grippy socks that keep touching my toes wrong from the stupid seams. Homesick, homesick for my family, homesick for my home that is in the form of my husband. Here, I'm safe; they are safe.

Mommy's absence has been explained as being in the hospital, sick. Sickness is an understatement. I lasted one day before carving my arms like a Thanksgiving turkey. I knew not to push the blade too deep. Blood still runs down my arm; bandages contain the rest, so our children are saved from any worry.

Hoodie covers bulky bandages. My husband knows something is wrong the minute he walks through our doors, as I wince from the contact. Yanking my sleeves up, I'm back to the ER, admitted yet again. The need to feel something is deep in my cells, my thoughts, and the desire to live is vacant.

Ghosts like the people who said they loved me. Where are they? Where's this support system people speak of? Where are the offers to help? Where are the people who claim to love my children and love me? I'm NOT hard to love, my children are not horrible children. Where in these godforsaken baby books did it mention we would be doing this by ourselves?

Cries for help are ignored, pleading goes unanswered, with the statement, "You wanted children, so raise them". People wonder why post-partum suicide rates are so high. Lack of postpartum care, lack of available mental health physicians (especially in small towns), hinder any chance of proper postpartum care. Tack on the lack of family or friend support, and it's a recipe for disaster.

Home again, I make it 2 days. Sitting on the bathroom floor, tears streaming down my face as I grab the comfort of a blade that used to comfort me as a teen. I relapse from self-harm, yet again. Years washed down the drain after last week's carving.

They say to call your tribe when you need help, but what about when the tribe is just you?

No one answers your calls; no one texts back. No phone calls to check in on you, check on the kids. Just the text of "Can I get a cute picture of the little one today? Is the little one holding her head up yet?" You find your tribe during the most challenging times of your life. You find out who's there and who's not.

Those days without sleeping with a colicky baby, a fussy toddler, or a pre-teen attitude. You pick yourself off that floor, hide the blade, and wrap your wrists. No post-partum depression is the same. Cry, walk away when the crying becomes too much. Wrap your arms around yourself and keep going.

This time, this time I have new piercings, hair is chopped, colored, and new tattoos. Nurses don't even recognize me as I state my name. Piercings are forced out due to some type of incident that happened within these walls. They stripped me of anything I was holding onto.

Fingernails are cut short from the staff; safety precautions they are now taking. Can they fix my mind this time? Can they take away these thoughts of self-hatred? I don't want to feel this way. I hate myself. Do I even remember joy? Do I remember what happiness means? There's this hollow feeling of numbness that overpowers all feelings.

My husband came to visit, words I never thought he would say, "You need to come home, stop treating this like a vacation".

I guess if you weren't born with a vagina, you wouldn't understand this hell you never asked for. Do I hold it against him? No! Yet here I am storming out of the meeting room where nurses are watching, watching for shit to hit the fan. Let me tell you, I ran to my "room" yelling, crying hysterically.

Nurses begged and pleaded for me to tell them what happened. What set me off? Yet all I wanted was for him to leave, never to speak to me again. Those words pierced me more than anything ever could.

Does he realize the hell I was living in? Did he realize I didn't want these thoughts? I didn't ask for this. I want to feel happiness again. I want to be home with my babies, not this fucking hospital.

Nurses escorted him out of the building; meds were given, yet my vision was filled with red, pure rage and hurt. Guess I got what I asked for, feelings. A short nurse comes over with a needle filled with medication; I'm being held down to be sedated. Didn't they know? Didn't they hear me?

This. A. Vacation?

No mother asks for these feelings; these are feelings I would never wish for even my worst enemy. Everything goes quite as my body caves to the drugs that were running through my bloodstream.

No phone calls home, no communication, I go silent. Festering with the feelings of rejection and lack of understanding. My world shattered with that statement, along with my heart.

Past these walls, an hour away, family was filling his head with "You need to divorce her, you need to take your daughter from her. She can't be a good mom".

People who have zero experience with post-partum. Good for them! Good for the people who can cast judgment on something they have never had to go through.

My stay here is over, back to living with my parents. Can one be even more broken? I want to go home; I want to feel his arms around me. Yet here I am, raising my children away from their other siblings. Calls and texts have gone unanswered. Never would I have thought these new feelings of despair would be sitting in my heart.

Granted, the urges to kill myself have faded. New feelings, however, have taken its spot.

Checking messages. Messages that I re-read. Will Brad come back to me? Can we go back to the way things were before post-partum changed who I was? Can I ever feel happiness again? Can we rebuild what we had, become stronger than we were before? Questions that eat at my brain, consuming me.

Brad didn't give up, he researched, studied, read up on Postpartum. All those messages I ignored have since been replied to. I can't let what we have vanish. We talked late into the mornings, showing up with flowers, and picked me up for dates. That love never died; it didn't abandon me like so many people have in the past. We both put in the work with counseling, marriage therapy, and lots of work as individuals.

Postpartum is not one size that fits all. It's ugly, tarnishing everything in its path.

People seem to have this misunderstanding that it will never happen to them, even if they have had one or several children. It can happen to those who have never struggled with depression or had postpartum depression with any of their prior births. Postpartum does not discriminate or choose when it hits.

We worked hand in hand, and the "I'm Sorry, I didn't understand" conversations were heartfelt.

Marriage counseling paired with individual therapy helped us see each other's sides.

When I stopped seeing it as: "This is what I'm going through," and saw it as: "This is what we are going through," It helped tremendously.

Those little tweaks of changing our perspective can make an impact on your marriage and mindset.

In no way, shape, or form am I saying this is everyone's struggle; every struggle is unique.

Overcoming post-partum psychosis was no easy feat for him or me. Let alone our children, who had no idea what was happening. Why was Mommy in the hospital? Why were they apart from their other siblings, or why was Daddy home but not Mommy? Brad had his own struggles with holding the weight of the home, children, and work. These battles are hard on every family.

Do not guilt yourself if you need help; there's no shame in reaching out for help.

Christmas music filled our home, baked goods enveloped the air, and our children's laughter bounced off the walls. Shopping was completed; presents were wrapped.

Morning of, our children bounded into our room with Christmas cheer that filled my heart. Little coos from between us as stepping even a few feet from her riddled me with anxiety. Hands enveloped ours while they led us to the toys under the tree.

My focus stayed on my babies, my babies that

needed me. Prescriptions were finally starting to do their job, making me feel better, almost normal.

Life went back to normal, almost like it didn't happen.

Swept under the rug. Meds, doctor's appointments, which are all tacked on. It became our new normal. Somewhere along the way, the feelings of despair had lessened. Feelings of wanting to kill myself were dead, much like if I had completed my fate.

Those precious faces looked at me with so much love and care. They were my soul's purpose for overcoming the darkness the brain tells me.

Life can be dark, life is hard, relentless, but we prevail.

If walking into urgent care or a hospital is what you need, do it.

There's no handbook on postpartum depression, but there are support groups, online support groups; your local OBGYN clinic might also have support groups available. Your feelings are valid and real! Remember that you matter; you're not a failure, and your story does not end here.

FAST FORWARD 7 years we purchased our first home. An accomplishment we worked our asses off for, for a secure future for our children. Overcoming the hard times is a testament to yourself and what you're capable of overcoming. We have raised some amazing children; most are now adults. A few have grown up and moved out to make their own way in this world. My post-partum is a thing of the past that comes to the forefront of my mind periodically. It's not sadness, it's triumph and pride in myself for making it further than I ever thought possible. Our marriage is stronger than it ever has been. We take all the wins we get; we love hard and overcome things we never imagined we would. This is my testimony of coming out the other side when my brain, body, and soul never thought we would survive. Yet here I stand 10 years later with so much love in my heart.

Depression still creeps in from time to time, reminding myself that I'm able to feel those feelings for the day, but tomorrow I'm pulling myself out of bed. Being present and putting one foot in front of the other that has truly helped me. This might not be what works for you. Running, gym, getting pulled into a book, hot bath, spending time with your animals, whatever self-care looks like for you.

Saying "No" is a full sentence. That goes for family asking for help, your supervisor asking you to cover an extra shift.

Remember, remember Momma, your powerful body is healing from bringing a beautiful baby into this world. At the end of the day, a job is just that. You are a body that fills a position. Are they going to pick you up off the floor when you're contemplating taking your last breath? Are they going to clean up the blood from your floor after grabbing the razor? This is the time to put yourself first, put your baby first!

Is the house a mess? It will be there tomorrow. What won't be there if you refuse to take the time you need is you? Your child(ren) won't have the mom they need. There's this quote somewhere in the abyss: "They don't need a perfect mom; they need a present mom".

Those days when taking a shower is too much, brushing your hair is something you did days ago. Changing your PJs becomes almost unbearable. Remember, remember you matter, your life matters, and your story does not end here!

Somewhere out there, a mom is going through something similar. Sitting on her bathroom floor, tears streaming down her face, wishing someone could hear her, wishing arms would wrap around her with whispers that she would be okay.

You will be okay, Momma.

These feelings won't last forever.

They feel so heavy because they are. Remember before you had that little bundle of joy, the smile that lit up a room when you walked in. Those late-night belly laughs, you remember those? Hunching over with your arms wrapping around your waist from those laughs that tore out of your gut. Yeah, you're starting to remember. Can I tell you a secret? The ONLY thing that made me laugh when I was pregnant with my son was watching YouTube videos of men being kicked in the balls. Yup, you read that right. It was the funniest shit ever and still is.

What movie is your favorite? Moana? Beauty in the beast? Pick your favorite movie, hit play with your favorite snacks within arm's reach, and take this time to unwind. These moments won't last forever. Even they feel like you will never feel happiness ever again. If I had taken my life 10 years ago, as planned, I would have missed three of my kids graduating from high school. My youngest drawing her amazing artwork. Our oldest son, becoming a pilot. Our boys growing into themselves and finding their own happiness. Kids who wouldn't have a mom cheering them on. Parents who would have buried 2 kids by this time. You feel like everyone would be better off without you... But I promise we all need you here with us. You don't end your pain; you pass it on.

Please keep going, Momma!

Remember, it takes 6 months for your body to

regulate back to itself. Postpartum and postpartum psychosis can take up to a year or longer.

> ***"The bravest thing I ever did was continuing my life when I wanted to die."***
> *Credit to Juliette Lewis*

I'M PROUD OF YOU!

2
VENGEANCE WEARS A CROWN

GINGER MOONWITCH

Gang Rape (not detailed), Betrayal of a family member, Murder, Blood

All characters are over the age of 20

CHAPTER 1

Their laughter bounces off the foliage of the forest and echoes in my ears as pain erupts through my body again. I've lost track after the third male. Sticks and stones press into my naked torso as the guard who once swore a vow to protect me defiles me.

My ass and pussy are screaming in agony. Blood and cum blending into one fluid as I'm helpless to their assaults. I can feel his gaze on me as his loyal followers run a train on me. As if I'm not the princess to the throne. The throne they devoted their lives to protect.

Each breath is a chore, and I'm sure a few of my ribs are broken. Whether it happened during the beating or as they take turns raping me, I'm not sure.

When I woke up this morning, I was normal. A grieving daughter, the next in line to lead the kingdom. But that all changed in a heartbeat when my uncle asked me to go for a ride in the forest. Though I would have never guessed he'd do something as vile as this.

Once the castle was out of view, his soldiers flanked us. Fear crept in immediately, but there was nothing I could do. I have no training. My whole life I've been pampered and spoiled. The darling princess.

I always suspected my uncle had ulterior motives. Especially after my mother died 5 years ago. He showed up out of the blue. The king's long-forgotten brother. Now it all makes sense.

My uncle was trying to weasel his way back into the family. So when my father stepped down or passed, the crown would be his. It must have been a kick in the nuts when my father used his last breath to hand everything to me.

The crown.

The safety of our people.

The kingdom.

After my mother passed away, everyone watched as my father's health declined rapidly. We knew his death was coming. He was never the same after his queen died. Now, a week after I laid him to rest, I'm on the path of the same fate.

The man thrusting like an animal into my limp body lets out a groan, pulling me out of my dissociated daze. His body twitches as his cum joins the other loads inside me.

A twig crunches as my uncle steps forward and crouches down in front of me. His fingers tangle in my hair and wrench my head up. I can barely open one eye from the swelling. The taste of blood still lingering in my mouth from the split in my lip.

"This could all have been avoided if your stupid father had given me my birthright from the start. I would have made sure you were married off to a nice man. You would have popped out a couple brats and pretended to be happy. This is a man's world. Women are not meant to rule. Everything I have done is for the kingdom, for the people."

He brushes a knuckle down my swollen cheek, and I flinch. A sinister chuckle leaves my uncle's lips as he tightens his hold on my hair. "Don't worry, Princess, you'll see your parents soon."

I'm helpless as he lifts me by my hair. The pain blends in with the rest that has consumed my body. A whimper leaves me as he forces me to my knees and grips my chin. "Look at them. Look at the men who destroyed you. Remember my face. You are nothing but a hole. A warm place. The people would have perished if you sat on the throne."

I scan the faces of the six men standing in front of me, committing them to memory. The torn fabric of my dress blowing in the gentle breeze that caresses my naked skin. Even after everything they've done, their hungry eyes devour my flesh.

One pulls a dagger from the sheath on his hip and steps forward. My uncle leans down, his hot breath ghosting my ear. "Burn in hell, dear niece."

The soldier plunges the dagger deep into my

side; the blade sliding between ribs as I choke on a gasp. Blood gushes from my wound as the man yanks the dagger out. My uncle releases my hair and I slump to my side in the dirt.

"Let's head back. I have a coronation to prepare for," he says with a laugh. The others join in as they mount their horses.

The sound of hooves fades as my vision blurs. My breathing shallow as I bleed out in the middle of the forest. Memories of happier times flash through my mind as I cling to the small scrap of consciousness. The sun sets on the horizon as the moon rises to take its place.

I close my eyes as I give up on the fight to survive. Everything is pointless. Women are nothing but a womb and a body to warm the bed.

My body feels light as I drift between life and death. Something warm lifts me off the cold forest floor. The musky scent of brush and mud fills my nose as I rest my head against the hard mass.

"This is not how your story ends," a deep voice says as everything goes black.

CHAPTER 2

My head throbs along with the rest of my body. I thought death was painless. That once you pass on, everything fades. Sucking in a breath, I hiss as my side burns.

"Don't move; you're safe here," the deep gravelly voice I heard before I passed out says. My heart races as I try to open my eyes. "Hold on, I'm going to wash your face, okay?"

I dip my chin slowly, then a warm cloth wipes my swollen eyelids. The heat and wetness feels soothing and peaceful, unlike the thoughts flooding my mind. The cloth leaves my face sooner than I'd like, and I slowly open my eyes.

A wooden ceiling greets me, and I turn my head. From what I can see, I'm in a small hunting cabin. A fire burns in the hearth as a massive male adds wood to it. An iron stew pot hanging from a chain above the blaze. Panic takes over, but I can't force my muscles to cooperate.

"Try not to move; you've been out for two days. The bleeding has stopped and there are no signs of infection." The man turns to face me and sits in the armchair by the hearth.

He's not handsome like most princes or males that I've seen at the castle, but his ruggedness gives him some appeal. Long brown hair frames his face, with most of the mass piled into a bun on top of his head.

Scruff covers his lower jaw, and a long scar runs down the right side of his face. It makes his dark brown eyes look more menacing. He's wearing a fur coat and leather pants. A dagger on his hip reflects the fire's glow.

"Wh-who are…" Before I can finish, coughs rack my body. My already sore lungs are on fire. He gets up and retrieves a bottle of water, moving towards me. His large hand cups the back of my head, and he lifts me up as the bottle opening meets my lips. The cool water tastes heavenly as I sip back my fill. The man rests my head back down and returns to his chair.

"My name is Ivan. I am a mercenary, or an assassin for hire, if you will. You are in my hideout; do not worry, no one will find you here. It's deep in the forest and only I know the location," he whispers.

The information helps me relax, and I look around the rest of the room. A lamp sits on the table behind the small couch my body is draped on. I can see an open door that leads to the bedroom. Unlike buildings in the kingdom, there's no electricity.

I look down at my body; a thick wool blanket covers me, and I slowly lift it to see I'm wearing a large shirt. Bile rises in my throat at the thought of another man seeing my body without permission.

"I only cleaned you up and treated your wounds. The dress has been burned, and I swear on my honour, I did not touch you unless it was necessary," he explains, answering my questions before I can even ask them.

"Thank you." My hands tighten on the blanket as I relax.

"Of course. Do you want to tell me why you were left for dead in the forest, princess? I don't need details, but I won't lie and say I'm not curious why I found you half dead in the middle of nowhere." Ivan leans back in his chair and crosses an ankle over his knee.

"Stella, not princess," I whisper and turn my head to face him. "Are you aware of what's happening in the kingdom?"

Ivan gives me a nod. "I'm sorry about your father."

Emotional pain mixes with the physical. I can't handle both right now, so I shut it down, pushing my feelings back into a box and sealing it shut. "My uncle was not pleased that I'd take the throne. He wanted it for himself, so he had to make me disappear."

"He did this to you?" Ivan grits out, his fists clenching on the armrest of his chair. Anger seeps from him like a tidal wave. But it's not directed at me, it's for what was done to me.

"Yes. Him and six others. Soldiers who must

have pledged their allegiance to him." My voice cracks, and I turn my gaze away.

"So, what are you going to do? Quick and to the point, or drag it out?" Ivan asks matter-of-factly. Like killing someone is as easy as hunting an animal.

Well, I suppose it is to him.

"What do you mean? I'm sure the citizens think I'm dead. He's probably already been crowned; I don't understand how I'm alive. There's nothing I can do," I snap.

"Bullshit," Ivan barks and stands from his chair. "Are you really going to let him get away with this? That throne belongs to you. YOU are supposed to rule the people, not that fucking piece of shit."

"Why do you care?" I try to yell, but the pain from my stab wound shoots through my body, stealing my oxygen. Ivan curses under his breath and inhales deeply. The tension leaves his body, and he steps forward with the water again.

He helps sit me up, arranging the blanket and pillow to make me comfortable. Ivan hands me the water and returns to his chair by the fire. "You're still healing. I apologize Stella, I shouldn't get you worked up. But I cannot sit here and listen to you demoralize yourself."

My hands tremble as I lift the bottle to my lips and drain half of it. "What you're suggesting is easy for you. Being an assassin and a man. Me? Not so much. Women can't be assassins. No one takes us seriously. For generations, men have pushed us around."

"So change it!" Ivan says firmly. "You have royal blood. What would you do if one of your people came to you with this issue?"

My mind goes blank as I stare at him. "I... I..."

"Would you stand by as a woman confesses the horrendous acts her husband or any man did to her? Would you tell her that her job as a woman is to take it?" Ivan asks, his voice levelled and controlled.

"Of course not! I would investigate and see that she gets justice."

"And who gets justice for you? Do you think your uncle would care about women's rights the same way you would? Grow a backbone and stand up for yourself," Ivan says with a huff and looks towards the fire. Standing up, he stirs the stew as we sit there with the topic hanging between us.

I can't argue with him. He has a point. If I do nothing, then I'm condemning women to the same fate. The problem will never stop unless someone ends it once and for all.

Ivan holds a bowl of stew in front of me, snapping me out of my thoughts. I take it and set the hot wooden bowl on my lap. "Thank you."

"Look, I'm sorry to upset you. But once you're healed, if nothing is done, then this act goes unpunished," Ivan says gently and sits on the other side of the couch, leaving some distance between us.

"If you had the knowledge and training to take your uncle down, would you?" he asks and turns his gaze on me.

My eyes are fixed on the thick, meaty meal in my lap as I process his question. The silence stretches between us, but Ivan doesn't push me. This type of decision isn't one to make without thinking it through.

Birds chirp outside the cabin as we sit there. The steam from the stew disappears as I think through every answer. Taking a deep breath, I turn my swollen gaze on the mercenary beside me.

"Yes."

CHAPTER 3

Since the night I awoke in Ivan's cabin, things have changed drastically. Once I had healed, my training began. The only way I will succeed in getting my crown back is if I end my uncle.

It started with rigorous physical training. Running, building muscle, and adapting to harsh environments. Next, Ivan helped break the mental block. Whenever I tried to give up, he'd push me past the breaking point.

When my body and mind were ready, that is when skill training started. Hand to hand combat, weapons handling, and learning about the human body. Where to cut to drag out a death, and where to slice to end a life in a heartbeat.

Ivan has proven to me that not all men are bad. After I agreed to wanting to learn how to be an assassin, Ivan set the ground rules.

"I am not like most men. Just like you, I have been forged from pain. I was not always a killer, and my life was once cozy and free. Rule number one: your consent matters. Yes, I will push you to your limits, but that is because I see your potential. All you have to say is stop and I will."

"Rule number two: I will not touch you unless necessary. Even during training, if I have to fix your form or instruct, I will verbally let you know beforehand."

"Rule number three: if you have troubles, you come to me. From this point on, I am your handler. If your mind

gets dark, if you want to end your life, or if the demons are too loud, you will tell me. Communication is important."

It's almost been a year since the night I was left for dead. Our plan is to strike on the anniversary. I feel like the old me would be proud, and when I finally take my rightful place on the throne, it will be with a new meaning of equality.

I have plans to change society, and the old ways of life will be abolished. Women will no longer cower in the shadows of their husbands. They will not be abused and treated as mere slaves. The time for equal rights has begun, and I will fight for it until my last breath.

The fire pops, bringing me back to the present moment. My hands are numb from the chilly water since I zoned out while cleaning them. Blood from the deer I killed this afternoon turns the water a deep pink, and I watch the swirling liquid as it blends into one.

"You okay, killer?" Ivan says softly, and I snap my head towards him. He's by the fire, flipping a piece of the fresh venison on the grate he placed over the flames.

"Yeah, just spaced out for a moment." Grabbing a cloth, I dry off my hands and move to sit on my makeshift bed. Ivan offered to give me the bedroom, but I insisted on sleeping in the living room. It helps knowing the door to freedom is right there, and that nothing is in my way should I need to flee.

"Do I need to remind you of rule three?" he says, arching a brow.

"No, it was nothing bad. Just thinking about how far I've come." I cross my legs and pull them close to my body as I get comfortable. My muscles ache, but the soreness is a reminder I'm alive.

"Your parents would be proud of you, Stella." Ivan takes his seat by the fire, and I nod slowly in agreement.

"I know we don't discuss our past, but may I ask you a question?" I tug on my wool blanket, draping it over my lap.

Ivan's lip twitches in the left corner. A tell I've learned that means he's suppressing his emotions. "Supper will be another hour, so I don't see why not. What would you like to know?"

"Who were you before you became a mercenary? Or I guess the better question is, what made you choose the life of an assassin?"

Ivan takes a deep breath, his fingers on his left hand tapping on the armrest of his chair. One thing I learned is that everyone processes trauma differently. I have told Ivan bits and pieces of what happened the night my uncle tried to kill me. He has never pushed for more and only takes what I'm willing to give. I owe him the same amount of respect.

Over the year, we have grown closer. Our relationship shifted from trainer and trainee to friends. I've developed feelings for the massive male that saved me, but I'm still working out my traumas and healing. Maybe one day things could be more, but until then, we respect each other's boundaries.

"Do you remember the fall of Svenia?" At my nod, Ivan continues. "I was almost 20 years old. My parents were the king and queen."

He gives me a moment to process the information; my eyes widening slightly, but I don't interrupt.

"When the castle was taken, soldiers slaughtered my parents. They believed I died in the crossfire, but in reality, one of my maids ushered me to safety. A retired mercenary took me in and trained me."

My hands tighten around the blanket in my lap as the news spirals around in my brain. "You were the prince. I wasn't very old, but I learned about the fall of Svenia. One thing I never understood was why. My parents were on good terms with the monarch."

Ivan grunts and stands from his seat, flipping the venison again. "Do you know who was responsible for the ambush?"

"No. From what I remember, it was a rogue platoon of soldiers that were upset by recent changes."

"Your uncle was the reason. Just like he poisoned the minds of your father's guards, he spoiled theirs," Ivan explains. "Your uncle is a cockroach. He feeds on power in whatever form he can get. Don't worry, his downfall belongs to you. I just want to watch him bleed."

My lips curl up into a sinister smirk. "Oh, he will definitely bleed."

"Yes, he will, killer. My demons will finally be put to rest, and all because of your hand." Ivan stares into the flickering fire as the revelation hangs in the air.

"And before you jump to conclusions, that was not why I saved you. When I stumbled across you in the forest, I saw myself. I knew that if you'd survived, you would change the nation. When you woke up, my theory was confirmed." Ivan turns to face me, and I can see the truth of his words reflected in his gaze.

"You know my plans for when I take the throne. It will not be easy, and I do not trust anyone. But I trust you. The people will take time to accept a woman ruling on her own," I say calmly, my eyes locked with his.

"When I take the crown, I want you by my side. Not just as a guard, but as the king. Your bloodline deserves to sit on the throne again."

Ivan's eyes widened in shock, his mouth opening to protest, but I cut him off. "Now, before you jump to conclusions, I am not doing this out of pity. You deserve this. Both of us have been forged through pain. We have both been through hell and have risen from the ashes."

I flick the blanket off my lap and get up, moving to stand in front of him. "I want you by my side, as my king. Ruling beside me like you should have ruled Svenia. Together, we can both change the old ways and see that the future monarchs have a kingdom to protect."

Ivan smiles gently and lifts his hand. He knows I'm sensitive to touch and hovers his hand over my cheek. "If that's what you want, then yes. I will rule by your side and I vow to protect you with my life."

CHAPTER 4

The streets are empty as Ivan and I make our way towards the castle. Sticking to the shadows, I jog on the balls of my feet behind him. Of course my ostentatious uncle would throw a party on his one year as king.

My black cloak billows around my ankles, and I can feel the damp condensation from my breath on the face mask. Only my eyes are uncovered. The hood of my cloak hides my hair, and I blend in with the night.

Ivan is wearing a similar outfit, though his swords slap against his knees from their sheaths on his hips. I prefer a more up-close and personal approach. During my training, I favoured the sharp dagger wrist attachment.

The cool metal of my weapons on my forearms helps ground me. The small rings on my middle fingers have a wire that releases my blades when I'm ready.

We reach the castle grounds and duck into a servants' tunnel. The perk of growing up encased within these walls is that I know all their secrets. Every hidden room, each forbidden passage, I know this place like the back of my hand.

As we reach the end of the tunnel, I can hear the muffled sounds of the party happening in the ballroom. Ivan pauses and turns to face me, his dark eyes boring into mine. "You're sure the kitchen is behind this door?"

"Yes, I used to play in this passage as a child." I adjust my mask and make sure my hair is tucked in.

"Okay, killer, I trust you. This is your show, I'll watch your back," Ivan whispers. For a moment we stand; this can either go in our favour or we both end up dead.

We spent the entire week going over the plan. From the informant Ivan spoke to, the six loyal dogs always stand behind my uncle's throne. Our best bet is to stay invisible and get behind them. There's another passage we can take, but to get there we have to pass through the kitchen.

Once in position, everything will have to move quickly. I have to destroy my uncle and reveal my identity before the other guards swarm in, all while staying alive.

Ivan steps aside, and I approach the door, pressing my ear to the wood. I hear nothing, so I gently push it open. The kitchen is empty, but I'm not sure for how long. Giving Ivan a nod, I slip out and stick to the wall as I tiptoe through the room.

He's right behind me as I reach the entrance to the kitchen and poke my head out into the hallway. I hurry down the hall and to the framed portrait of the kingdom. The photo takes up the full wall, and I wiggle the wooden frame until it opens. A dark stone passage hides behind it and we scurry inside.

Ivan shuts the passage, and we wait for our eyes to adjust before moving.

The sound of music and muffled voices gets louder as we reach the end of the hidden tunnel. This stone door is the only thing between me and my birthright. "Okay, this is it. The throne is eight feet in front of this door."

Ivan reaches out but stops just before he touches me. At my nod, he grips my shoulder softly. "You have trained for this moment. I will take care of the guards you don't get. Just focus on your uncle. Show them you are alive and powerful."

"Thank you, Ivan, for everything." I put my hand on top of his and squeeze lightly.

I turn to face the door, my fingers twitching to release my blades. My mind clears with each calming breath I take as I build up the courage. Placing a hand on the door, I take one last deep breath before shoving it open.

Flexing my fingers, my two knives extend from my wrists as I lunge out of the hidden passage. One of my nightmares whips his head towards me, and I plunge my weapon into his throat and rip it out quickly. Blood sprays my face, the metallic liquid soaking my mask.

Ivan's massive frame blurs beside me as he takes out 2 guards at once. Both swords move through the air in a whisper, slicing through their abdomens.

The crowd screams in fear as I lock eyes on my uncle.

His fur mantle is unnecessary, and on his head is my father's crown. I see red and screech as I attack. In two strides I reach the throne and grip his hair before he can stand, placing my dagger against his throat.

I can feel his Adam's apple bob against the metal as he gulps. Time slows to a crawl; guards shout and push through the crowd as everyone scrambles to escape. I can hear bodies drop to the floor behind me as Ivan works. "Hello Uncle."

Shock, confusion, and fear passes over my uncle's face as he pieces everything together. He opens his mouth to speak, but I don't give him the chance.

"Burn in hell." My voice is ice-cold, menace and vengeance lacing my words. I slice across his throat, a gush of blood spilling down his chest, soaking the formal suit and mantel.

Everything is silent. For the first time in a year, I feel peace.

Keeping my grip on his hair, I saw through his neck as my uncle gurgles and flaps his arms around. My knife cracks through his spinal cord, and his body drops. All eyes are on me as I lift his head up and take in the look of terror frozen on his face.

Nobody moves as I round the throne and kick his body out of the way. I flick my middle fingers and both blades slide back into my sleeves as I take a seat on MY throne. Ivan steps up beside me, and I prop my uncle's severed head on my knee. His blood soaking through my cloak and pants.

Ivan reaches out, and when I nod, he pulls down my hood and mask. The whole room gasps as I toss my head from side to side, releasing my silver hair from its confinement. With my free hand, I take my father's crown off my uncle's head and place it on mine.

"Citizens, I am sure you are all wondering what is happening. Let me clear everything up. My dear uncle here tried to kill me. His greed for power consumed him. But I have finally come to take my rightful place on the throne."

"Beside me is the lost prince of Svenia. Just like me, my uncle tried to destroy him. Take this as your only warning: anyone loyal to my uncle has until the sun rises to leave my kingdom. If you stay, you will be executed." I pause and give everyone a minute to process. I know it will take time. Things do not change overnight.

But if I can crawl back from hell and rise from death, then anything is possible. Ivan holds out his hand and I place mine in his, our fingers intertwining. We stand as a united front before our subjects. His deep voice booms around the room.

"Bow to your queen."

3
RACING HER ROCK BOTTOM

A TWISTED

Drug Addiction.

Child Neglect.

Mention of death.

1 NOT ON MY WATCH

"What are you doing here?" Amy says when I bust through her door like a bat out of hell.

"Pack a bag!" I bark, charging past her.

"What? Why?"

"Where's Symon?" I ask, ignoring her as she follows on my heels.

"He's napping. Seriously, what's going on?"

"Why are you not packing a bag?"

"You're scaring me."

"I don't care! Pack-a-freaking-bag!" I snap as I beeline for Symon's bedroom.

The peaceful little thing is sleeping. Rosy cheeks, drool in the corner of his lips. Completely unaware of the chaos about to ensue. I scoop him up gently, bringing his blanket with me and wrapping him in a cocoon.

"Shh, shh, Aunt Lindsay's got you."

On my way back out of the room, I find Amy standing in the doorway.

"Bag now," is all I say.

With terror-filled eyes, she stops questioning and rushes to her room. While she's busy grabbing her things, I put Symon in his car seat. His diaper bag is closed, and in one fell swoop, it's over my shoulder. I scoop him up, still sleeping and call out for my best friend.

"Move bitch! We don't have time to dawdle."

Amy clamours down the hallway, still shoving things into her duffel bag.

"Holy shit, I'm coming. Keep your panties on," she gripes before stopping at Symon's room to grab a stuffed Elephant and waving it at me in defence. "Are you going to tell me what's going on?"

"In a minute. Come on. We got to go."

I lead the way, running as fast as the car seat will let me. Amy stays hot on my heels as we race outside and scramble down the sidewalk, one arm reaching for her son. It's not like I'm going to drop him, but the poor girl has no idea what to be afraid of.

That's when I see it. The black Sedan parked on the street. The woman stepping out with her clipboard, and the cop car pulling up behind her.

"Look out!" I say, shoving her through a bush.

I follow carefully behind her, blocking Symon from the branches and twigs with my own body.

"What the hell?"

"Shh. Be quiet," I point.

She follows my finger over to the social worker walking toward her front door.

"Wait, what. Why are they here?"

I hush her again. We are only a good twenty yards from the house. It would take one whimper from the baby to give us away.

I place the car seat in the garden bed and rock him slowly, "For the sake of all of us, you need to calm down."

She goes to say something, but I mouth, *'Be quiet!'* and glare.

Her shoulders sink, and she watches as the officers pitter around her yard. The worker peeks in her windows and writes things down.

"This isn't fair. I was going through his stuff because he's growing so fast. Of course, our rooms are going to be a mess."

"That's not what they're looking for."

"How would you know?"

Her chest rises higher with every breath, likely from the anxiety raging through her. Be it because she's innocent or because Stacy told the truth. Either way, the panic is justified. It's why I bit my tongue when she nips at me. Scared dogs bite.

I nod my head to the right, motioning for her to get moving, "Stay low. And keep behind this bush until we can get around the corner."

"Where's your car?" She sniffles.

"Quint has it today," I answer, wishing I could whisk her away from all this.

"Why did he need it? What's wrong with his truck?"

"Good question."

2 NO SUCH THING

I didn't want to seem paranoid. I knew how ludicrous it sounds, but me not having a car on the same day Nikki made her move has me on edge. Call me a conspiracy theorist, but I don't trust it. *Why did Quint need my car today? Was he in on it?* I shake my head, eyes locked on the sleeping baby on the floor of a dirty bus. *How could they do this?*

"So if you just got the call, how did you get to my place so fast?" Amy asks from across the aisle.

"I ran."

"Dude, that's like 2 miles. What do you mean you '*ran*'? Was there no cab you could've hailed, or something?" She waves her hands around the bus we're taking back to my place.

"I tried. Nobody picked me up, and the bus never would have gotten me there in time. So I started running, alright? Is that okay with you? Maybe next time you'll answer your damn phone." I half-tease, though I mean every word.

"Oh shoot. Yeah, Symon was watching his baby shows and killed the battery. It's charging…" She pats her pockets and then digs in her bag for a moment. "Fuck. I left it there. We have to go back."

"Nope. Not if what I heard is true." *So much for waiting until we were home.* I pinch the bridge of my nose. "Somebody's going to be waiting for you to come back. If Stacy said what she says she did, you're going to lose custody of Symon."

"Why? What did she say? Nikki's behind this?! Wha..? No way. There's no way."

"We'll talk about it later. Now's not the time." I use my foot to rock Symon before he stirs, and avoid the nearby eyes gawking our way.

"This is so dumb. How could she? I thought—" Amy hiccups a sob and turns to hide away, gluing her eyes out the window.

I give her a moment and focus on Symon when my pocket buzzes.

"Speak of the devil, and they shall appear," I say when I see the caller ID.

I hold up my phone and show her it's Stacy calling.

"Let me talk to her."

"No. You're off the grid," I swat her away and put the phone to my ear.

"Hey, gir—"

"Who the fuck do you think you are?" I snap, cutting her off before she can fake being friendly.

Amy waves a hand, telling me to keep quiet. People are starting to stare, so I finish in a more hushed growl. "I mean, what kind of friend does that? You say you're here for her. You call yourself her *bestie*, then you go and do this? If she's struggling, it's our job as her friends to help her. Not destroy her. And you know for a fact that if what you did worked the way you wanted it to, she probably would have killed herself tonight.

Did you consider that? Like, let's be real. We've all been around each other since we were kids. We know each other's demons. Instead of helping her fight back, you stab her in the back."

"Lindsay. You don't know what I know. She doesn't tell you everything."

"I know that. You think I'm stupid. We live two different lives. We have different friends. Different *hobbies*, if you will. But so long as I am here. Amy will not fail. And no matter what you throw at her, I will be here to block it. Me. And last I checked, you don't want to take on that battle again.

"Oh, whatever, Lind's. I thought you were smarter than this. I thought you'd want what was best for her, what was best for Symon."

"I do. But the way you just tried to go about it is the wrong way. Having a child thrown into the system, that black hole, is the wrong way! She has a whole community around her; why would we not reach out to them first? Why can't we be a team and work together to save her little family? Why did you take it upon yourself to throw in the towel and give up on them? What gives you the right to ruin someone's life just because you don't agree?"

"Agree? With what? Oh my God. She's on drugs, Lindsay. Like, hard shit. She's doing it with him in the house."

"You've seen her do this?"

"Not personally. But there is evidence. I do this shit too. I know what the aftermath of a sesh looks like."

"So she's being reckless. Who's to say it's not from a night he's not home?" I demand, grasping at straws at this point.

"He's always home! And she can't go more than a few hours without it. Hell, I don't think I've seen her go 30 minutes. It's past reckless. She's getting dangerous. Symon is at risk. He needs to be put first."

I turned to Amy. The volume is loud enough that she can hear every word. She meets my eyes, but rather than shake her head and defend herself, she sank.

Fuck. Nikki's right. She's in deeper than I thought.

I suck my teeth. As much as I didn't regret going my route, it was clear things weren't going to be as cut-and-dry. Reinforcements will be needed.

Amy mouths, *Sorry,* but I brush it off.

"Listen, Nik. I get where you're coming from. But if that's the case, then we bring Symon into one of our homes while we get her some help. We don't send him off with strangers. We don't rip her world, and the only thing giving her purpose away from her."

"Purpose? If he gave her purpose, you'd think she'd get sober."

"Says the bitch always putting it in her fucking face. Are you dumb?"

"I don't tell her to do it!"

"Nah, not at all. That's like waving free chocolate in front of a child and expecting them not to reach."

"This is a waste of time. Do what you want, but she's not fit right now."

"I agree. Doesn't matter though!. We start within our group. If things don't get better, we go from there. We don't start with the extreme. I mean, where was the conversation? The intervention? You skipped all the steps!"

"Whatever you say. Apparently, you're the boss now, eh? So, go do what you're gonna do. Be her little hero. You have no idea what you're about to get yourself into."

"You might be right. But I gotta try, because unlike you, I'm not going to sit here and watch her fall. I'm sure as hell not going to push her off the edge!"

I hang up. *Shit. Maybe I should have gotten the whole story before racing over here.*

3 PRACTICE RUN

We barely say a word after I get off the phone. Even our waitress seems to feel our tension when bringing our drinks. There is no more swooning over Symon or friendly banter. She simply delivers our order and runs.

Amy sips her coffee, and I rack my brain over our next move. If I bring both of them home with me, it'll put my son at risk. Not to mention she'd never leave. I send out an S.O.S and pray Quint makes the right choice.

Eventually, I grab the diaper bag and start taking inventory. Two diapers and an empty packet of wet wipes. Wrappers and…

"Ew," I hold up a chunky bottle to show Amy. "You have nothing in here. What did you pack?"

"Uh, clothes, mostly."

"And?"

"Makeup."

I toss the bottle back in the baby bag and yank hers up from under the table.

"This is all your clothes. Oh, and this." I hold up a singular onesie with a stain.

"I figured you'd grab him things."

"I told you to pack a bag."

"Yeah, but I thought—"

"You're a mom!" I put up my hands in surrender. "I'm sorry. But c'mon."

"I'm sorry."

"Don't be sorry to me. Be sorry to him."

I point and find Symon's big blue eyes staring at me. He is perched on the table, still stuck in his car seat.

"Hey, buddy. You're up."

"Hey, baby." Amy Cooes, handing him his elephant rather than picking him up.

"We need to get him some stuff before we go to my place," I say, putting everything away.

The diner is suddenly too small. The air is thick and hot, and since opening the diaper bag, it's all I can smell: sour milk, pee, and mouldy snacks. *I need air.* My toes start tapping, and I close my eyes. *Oh, holy shit what did I get myself in?*

"Let's go." I place cash on the table.

"Our food just got here."

"Nothing he can eat."

"Can we at least get it to go?"

I grab Symon and his bag, leaving Amy to fend for herself. If she's going to be selfish, then she can take care of herself. For now, at least.

"I can't believe this is happening," she whines when she finally meets me outside, doggy-bag in hand.

"What did you think would happen?"

"Look, I get that I fucked up. I do. I promise I do. But I was getting it under control. And I've only done it once while he was home. Literally this past weekend! And I've been beating myself up since."

"Mmhm." I nod, leading the way down the street.

At this point, I don't know what to believe. Addicts will say anything. They will spin a story to make it seem less 'bad'. If she's admitting she's done it once, there is a good chance it's been more than that.

Don't get me wrong, I stand by my choice to keep Symon out of the system. They mean well, but it's traumatic for everyone involved. It was the 'not planning for her' that I'm second-guessing. If she was dabbling, sure. I'd bring her home and get it sorted. With her being a full-blown addict, I'm in need of some serious help.

Things are not about to go as smoothly as we both hoped.

We reach a pharmacy, and I pause. Inside or outside, she's going to make a scene. Best I rip off the band-aid now.

"I believe you." *No, I don't.* "But I'm going to be taking Symon with me tonight, ok? I will pull out Mac's old playpen, and tomorrow I will figure out something a little more permanent."

"Permanent?" She whispers, following me inside like a lost puppy.

"Semi-permanent." I nod."I'll take care of him while we get you back on your feet."

Her eyes don't leave Symon as I place him in a cart. She knows it's the right thing to do, but it won't be easy. I offer for her to push. That way, she can dote and love on him before she gets the rug pulled out from under her *again*.

"Who's we?"

She leans over the cart as we walk, stroking Symon's cheek and bopping his nose. He giggles, adoring his mother's smiles.

"Pardon?" I ask, heading straight for the baby section.

"You said '*while we get you better.*' Who is 'we'?"

"Well, depending on what Quint says, he and Bec will have you at their place while you detox. Bec, being a nurse, will be a big help. In a couple of weeks, we will find you a job, and by the time we let CAS get ahold of you, your shit will be in order."

"You make it sound so easy," she scoffs.

"Nothing about this is going to be easy. But those are the stages. The steps will vary; breaking it down might help it seem less scary. The detox will be *a* hard part. Staying away from it after will be your real challenge."

She shakes her head as if I think she doesn't already know this. Like I wasn't there through her last addition, her recovery and now, apparently, her fall off the wagon.

"What makes you think I can do this?"

"Because you did it once before."

"And failed."

"Consider it a practice run."

We both have a well-needed chuckle, and she stops to give me a deep hug.

"Thank you. I don't know what I'd do without you."

"You'd be on your kitchen floor bawling, or in the back of a police car with an assault charge for punching a case worker."

"Ha! You're probably right."

"I usually am."

4 REUNIONS

Eight days later…

As happy as I am to bring Symon over to finally see Amy, it's Quint I didn't want to see. He and his Husband, Bec, did a great job with her detox. She'd made it through the rough bit, and though she is worse for wear, she is doing much better.

Her voice on our call this morning had genuine life in it. I could almost feel her rosy red cheeks through the phone. She deserves to see her little man after working so hard, but damn, *why can't someone else take him over?*

"We're here," I chime, stepping in Quint's front door like I have since we were kids.

"We're in the living room." Bec greets.

"Oh, thank god, maybe he's not even here," I mutter, helping my son with his shoes before shuffling the car seat to the other room.

"Maybe who's not here, mommy?" Mac asks the moment we enter the living room.

I freeze and fake a smile, praying no one heard him. But before I could quietly fib an answer and keep him from repeating, Quint stood up.

"I think she means me, little man."

I press my lips between my teeth and look to the ceiling. *Cool, cool, cool. This makes it much less awkward.*

"Why?" Mac asks, but this time I just cover his mouth and grin.

"Enough questions for today. Go play." I nudge him in the direction of their son's toys.

Not looking in Quint's direction, I take Symon over to his mother. She's on the couch, weak and sore, but healthy. Bec hands her a steaming coffee and sits beside his patient.

"Say Hi to Mommy," I coo, pulling him from his seat and offering to put him on Amy's lap.

She doesn't reach out for him. Instead, Bec takes him and plops him down on his. Amy flashes a sad smile and holds up her coffee as an excuse.

"I'm still a little shaky. We'll cuddle later."

"Of course." I nod, knowing we're heading out in an hour.

I'm not sure if it was shame or guilt, but the glint of tears in Amy's eyes while she watches Bec entertain her bouncy boy has me wondering. After a weekend apart, I have to hold back on squeezing the air out of my kid. It's been over a week, and she almost seems… scared to touch him.

"Lind's?" Quint says, making me jump. "Can we talk?"

He nods his head towards the kitchen and walks away, expecting me to follow.

I sneer and roll my eyes. Amy snickers, knowing our history. While Bec's face scrunches in confusion.

"It's just to discuss our next move," Bec says naively.

"Sure it is." Amy shakes her head and sips at her mug.

Again, Bec looks at us, unsure.

"Amy can fill you in. I'm off to argue with my *big brother,*" I say sarcastically.

There is no blood relation; it's just the dynamic we've all developed over the years. He was in charge, the boss, but not quite strict enough to be deemed a 'dad'. Unlike me. I've been deemed the mother-goose since the summer of grade ten, when we all went on a drunken adventure, and my toppling-ass managed to get everyone home safe-ish.

Now, somehow, to this day, we are still sorting people's shit.

"You rang," I scath.

"You can't keep avoiding me." He says, crossing his arms and leaning on the counter.

"Sure, I can."

"Lindsay, I didn't know."

"Bullshit. You're the one who told me."

"When I found out—"

"Nah, that shit doesn't happen that quick. Nikki isn't going to just wake up and say, *'Oh, you know what I'm going to do? Cause shit.'* No, she's going to talk to someone. And from what I've gathered off the grapevine, is that you two have been sleeping together. Who would a woman confide in when it comes to something like this... oh that's right, her boytoy.

"Would you keep it down? Jeez"

"So it is true. You're sleeping with Nikki."

"Was. I'm not happy about any of this, either, Lind's."

I laugh under my breath. Not because it's funny, but because it's disgusting. He knows the sound well. He comes closer, eyes pleading for me to believe him.

"Nikki told me about the drugs and shit. Amy was selling herself, too, eh? Like, having strangers over to the house while Symon was sleeping. Or once, I guess he was awake. Amy bragged to Nikki that he was a perfect 'host'. Whatever that means. Hopefully not what I'm thinking it does."

"Are you serious?"

"Completely. Amy was falling hard. Nikki panicked. I told her to wait when she brought it up. I said we'd get everyone together and figure something out. Get Amy help. Just like how you told her on the phone—We talked that day too, by the way. And I agree with you. She took it too far, too fast. There are ways to do this, and she did it wrong. I agree with you. I told her she fucked up."

"Did you?"

"Yes!"

"And how'd the mistress take that?"

"Not well. And don't call her that. For fuck sakes, Lind's."

We each take a step back. He needs to breathe, and I need to crack my knuckles before popping him in the chin.

"You really told her off?" I ask, quickly peeking out to the living room.

"Yes. Then I called you and got my own earful." He shrugged sadly. "You know I love you guys like family. I'm not going to sit back and watch things fall apart."

"Then how did you know when you called me? Like, something's missing. You didn't know, but you still warned me. Actually! No you didn't. That shit slipped out mid-rant. If I hadn't answered, Symon would be in the system right now. And why that day to take my car? What was wrong with your truck, huh?"

"That was pure fluke. It was in the shop. I promise. That wasn't planned."

"Maybe not on your end. But your little side piece isn't stupid."

"No, she's not... Honestly, I didn't know she was going to do that. She said it in passing. I thought I had time to make a plan, bring everyone together, and figure it out. I really did. Then she just admitted to calling. As if it were any other service. No remorse, no fear. She was proud. Like she saved the day rather than made everything ten times worse."

"You should have said something the moment she brought it up. Hell, your dick could still be tacky and you should have pulled out your phone. Instead, you waited. Expecting that hot-headed, know-it-all bitch to wait on you." I shake my head, eyes wide. "You can't be that dumb."

"Holy shit, you're impossible."

"Whatever. You know, I honestly don't even care anymore. Let's just focus on getting her healthy so we can move on with our lives. See you at the summer reunion kind of thing, k?"

5 UNCANNY

I leave Quint in the kitchen, not allowing him to keep going around in circles. When, really, he had a warning he should have passed along. I sit on the floor next to Mac and Symon, who are playing beautifully like they have all week.

The two-year age gap doesn't bother them. Mac showed him toys and how to use them, practicing his words in the process.

"They're already like brothers," Amy says with a smile laced in sadness.

"They're friends. Life-long, just like all of us." I add as Quint stops in the doorway.

He knows he screwed up, and I know I'll have to let it go. Just not yet. *He should have told me…*

I change subjects, asking about her week and how things have been. There were a few text updates, but I want more. I want to hear Amy's plan when Symon rips a big one, filling the room with rancid baby stank.

Mac instantly pinches his nose and says, "Pee-yew!"

And we all lean away, laughing and waving away the smell.

"I'll do this. You've had to all week, and Mom's not ready yet." Bec offers.

"Thank you," Amy and I say together.

Once alone, Quint comes over and takes Bec's

seat on the couch. Amy reaches for Mac, but I scoop him into a hug and send him back toward the toys in the corner.

"Nice try. You're not using my child as a distraction."

"Yeah. We need to make a plan."

I tsk at his assumption. "Silly, silly man. You think I've just been sitting around playing house? You weren't the only one kicking ass this week."

Quint sucks his cheeks and leans back, leaving me to dazzle them with all I've been up to.

"Remember those stages I told you about?" I ask, turning my attention to the one that matters. "You've made it over the first hurdle. Now it's keeping yourself clean. And busy. So I got you a job. Norm's friend has a shop downtown. He said he'd try you out there."

"I can do pizza."

"Yes, you can. And I already got your house back in order. You'll be going into a fresh space. All you have to do is keep it tidy."

"Easier said than done with him. You've seen it. He doesn't stop moving."

"Well, that's where the *real* gut punch comes in."

Amy's breath picks up, and her eyes start to water. Quint doesn't hesitate and brings her in for a hug.

"Sorry. But we haven't even gotten to your N.A meetings yet—"

"We have those?"

"Yes. And you will be going twice a week. The new job will work around any random meetings you feel you need to go to."

"Ok. And Symon?"

"He will be staying with me. For now. Until you've been on your own for a while and get things under control. Then we can slowly add him back in," I promise. Amy sinks, and I reach out and take her hand. "This isn't forever. And I'm not saying you won't be seeing him whenever you want to. You can even have sleepovers at my place.

"Why are you treating me like I'm some kind of monster? I'm not going to hurt my own baby. I know I messed up, but I'm going to do better."

"We know you are."

"We do. I'm not trying to say you're anything. We just need to put Symon first. We need to play this the same way CAS would. That way, when they do get a hold of you, you have your shit in order. They see you've put things in place to protect him. They will see your effort and sacrifice.

"What if they don't?"

They will!

"So long as you do what Lindsay is saying, everything will work out. She clearly has shit under control. We just need to follow her lead."

I nod, "It's almost as if I should have been involved since the beginning, eh?"

"But what if I can't?"

"If you want to, you can. Anything you've ever wanted, you managed to get. Every-single-time. It's uncanny. So if you want this, if you want Symon, you'll figure it out."

"What if I don't *want* to? He deserves better, and I'll never be able to give him that. I can't keep doing this alone. I don't want to."

"You're not alone. You just need to reach out and ask for help—"

"Thank you, sir." I wave him away before he can mansplain her needs. "How about you go get her a drink and something to wipe her face. We're busy talking."

"Don't be mean. He's just as pissed off as you." Amy says as he leaves the room.

"I doubt it." I get up, take the communal-hugging spot and wrap her into my arms. "Listen, it's just you and me. Be honest. Do you want to be a mom?"

"What? Of course?" Amy pulls away and glares at me.

"Don't be mad, I'm just asking I was there when you talked about aborting—then when you tried to get him a daddy before he came out. If it's too much, you can say it. I struggle too, and I have somewhat of a village. I won't judge you if you need to step away. So long as you get sober, I don't care."

"What are you saying? I love him!"

"Of course you do. That's why you want better for him. You choosing not to be his full-time mom isn't you not loving him. It's you making the hardest decision a woman can ever make, ok? It's you breaking your own heart to protect his. Besides, Mac could always get a brother, and you can be 'mom', 'aunt', or my friend that comes by.

The more I talk, the more tears stream down her face. She's thinking about it. Genuinely thinking about it, and as heartbreaking as it is, if she does choose to opt out of being his mom, I'd find a way to make it work.

Quint is in the doorway. I'm not sure when he came back, but he hears my offer too, and by the nod he gives me, I know he'll help if needed.

"You don't have to make up your mind today. Our focus is getting you clean. He will be safe until then, and once you're clear-headed, that's when you can choose."

"But what if it takes years to get clean?"

"Then it takes years." I shrug, and the sobs she's been sucking break finally break free. "Babe. I'm so sorry. I know this isn't the time to shatter you. But it's going to be something to think long and hard about."

"I know you're right. But I don't know what to do." She sniffles.

"You're not supposed to. Everything you're feeling right now is based in guilt over what's happened. Don't make any choices until that mess is cleaned up. Do you hear me?"

"But—"

"But nothing. Symon is safe. That's all that matters."

FINALLY.

SADLY SYMON NEVER DID GO BACK TO Amy. The first year seemed promising, until she showed up to a BBQ thinking she was slick and that no one could tell.

That was strike one.

After that she seemed to go completely downhill. She'd taken the out I never should have offered, and gave up. She wouldn't even get sober for herself.

After a couple years, Symon went to live with Quint and Bec. They got a bigger house, and he was so used to spending half his time with them already. It was an easy transition, and Mac and I went to visit. We kept the family tight despite everything.

Then he turned six, and his grandparents finally came looking. I tried to connect with them several times, but it wasn't until they found out Symon was living with a Gay couple that they intervened.

It was a messy fight. Long and drawn out, and in

the end we lost. Blood relation will always win in the court of law. Honestly, we were just lucky we didn't get fined. Pretty sure Amy had to pay back the years of government child funding she wasn't entitled to, but the rest of us got off with a slap on the wrist and, encouraged to do it by the books next time—which there never was one.

Since they took custody, none of us have really seen Symon outside of random passings, and by the time he was old enough to say 'hi' to, he didn't know who we were. It's weird watching a child you helped raise grow up from a distance. While a mother tramps around instead of helping bring us back together. I still hate her for that.

It was not until a family friend's funeral that I got to see him again. He's 25 now. With a pretty girl on his arm and straight shoulders. I'm too shy to walk up, but Quint is here now, so I'll just follow on his bold coat-tails.

"Symon, is that you?"

"Hey… I know you."

"Yeah you do. It's me Quint. I used to take care of you."

"Yeah. I have old pictures of you. From the house Nana and Papa took me from."

My throat closes, and I'm so glad it's Quint up front.

"That was my house."

"Hey babe. Remember how I said I grew up in a

really cool house? This is the guy. Where's the other one?"

"Bec? My husband? He's here. He's giving his condolences. I had other priorities. How's it going, kid?"

"Good. Good. I work for an up-and-coming tech firm. We're engaged. Looking at houses. We're really good. Hey. Can I get your number? I was kind of hoping I'd find a way to get a hold of you today. Kind of why we came."

"Same," I admit.

"Hey." He reaches his hand out to shake mine. "I'm Symon. This is Jessica—Wait. I know you too. You're that crazy lady who's always got new games to try out."

"That's me." I choke on a happy sob.

"I remember you too." He nudges his finance, "This is my almost-mom. The mom I should have had. Can I get your number too?"

"Of course!" I burst, ready to wrestle someone for a pen and paper.

That is until Quint had to ruin it,

"Speaking of your mom. How's she doing, if you don't mind me asking?"

"No idea. I haven't talked to her in years. I stopped giving her my allowance and she stopped poking around. I got a call last year that she was in the hospital and needed her next of kin to pick her up. I just told them to take me off her call list. They won't, so I'm sure the next call I get will be about her being dead in a ditch somewhere."

"Symon." Jessica nudges him.

"What? They are the last people I'd have to sugar coat with. They've seen it first hand."

"I'm so sorry, Symon. We all wanted so much more for you." Quint sighs.

"She did too." I say, though I doubt he'd ever believe me.

"I don't need much more. I got pretty-well everything I need. And now that we're talking again, all that's next is a few kids and I'm set. Amy stopped being my mom a long time ago. It hurt, and sometimes it still does. But I can't let her bring me down."

"You sound like a good man there, Symon. I'm proud to see it." Quint pats his shoulder.

All I can manage is a squeak. "Me too."

"Wouldn't have happened if you didn't get me out of that house."

Again all I can do is nod. Quint keeps up the conversation, asking Symon more about his life and goals. I try to keep up, nodding when the time is right, but my head is somewhere else. My heart races and my face starts to tingle. *When will that call come,* I wonder silently, looking toward the casket and missing my best friend. *When will that be her…*

4

BROKEN DOLLY

YOUR GASLIT PLAY IS OVER

MARNEY CARROLL

DOMESTIC VIOLENCE, ABUSE

Breaking down the walls,
looking for a fight,
I'm fucking tired of crying,
howling through the night.

Hello? Can you hear me?
I'm fucking standing here!
I'm not just gonna go away,
I won't just disappear.

**I MURDERED YOU A THOUSAND TIMES,
ALL UP IN MY HEAD,
IF LOOKS COULD KILL — MY DARLING,
—
YOU'D CERTAINLY BE DEAD.**

*You won't take me for granted.
No way, not anymore
I'm not your fucking lackey.
I'm stronger than before.*

I don't need your "good opinion".

I have one of my own.

Please stay on your high horse

while I obliterate your throne.

I'm not your fucking punching bag.
It's me who's swinging now.
Your gaslit play is over.
Step up and take a bow.

YOU TAKE NO ACCOUNTABILITY
FOR YOUR PART IN ALL MY RAGE,
SO I'LL PURGE IT ALL OUT HERE
FOR YOU
IN THE SOLACE OF THIS PAGE.

5
NOT TODAY

VIVIAN RAGE

Grief

VIVIAN RAGE

My Doc Martens crunch steadily as my steps shift the small white shards of gravel that make up the pathway. I make a mental note to pick the tiny stones out of the tread of my soles later, as I balance a takeaway coffee in one hand and a large bunch of lilies in the other. I was lucky to find a florist that still had them: autumn had set in early this year, draining warm, sun-filled days into chilled overcast, leaching lush greens and bright blooms into tones of ochre, amber, and rust.

I hold the bouquet as far away from me as I can manage. My eyes are already itching something fierce, and my nose has turned itself into a dripping tap. Unfortunately, they were her favourites, and if I am honest, they are a gift of guilt. Visits have been few and far between; I avoid the places where I may run into the two that claimed to love her the most.

"Hello, my friend," I say as I lower myself to the bench; the old wood creaks under my weight. "If this thing breaks, I expect you will have a good cackle."

I lean forward and place the offensive flora into the jar of water that is always there, ready to receive offerings of love, grief, or apology. Her nameplate is filthy—the guilt twinges at me again. Do they even come here anymore?

I lightly brush the dead leaves and dust away, pull at some weeds that have crept in around it, and silently promise to bring something to clean it properly next time. Someone has painted her name in blue glitter at some point. Fitting, she used to shed the stuff like the fur of a white cat on a black jersey.

I take a deep breath. Hold. Breathe out.

My voice sticks in my throat. I feel a bit silly talking to buried ashes when I do not think a living person can understand.

But it is not that she is dead, is it? It's that in life she was my anchor, my rock, and my light in the storm. I do not think death can change that.

I stare at the rosemary growing like wildfire around her stone, overtaking the bare spaces that surround it, filling the air with its sharp and familiar scent. We planted it the day we laid her to rest beside her mum. Her sister and I, that is, back when we still claimed each other as family. A symbol of love and remembrance. An evergreen to keep her enveloped in colour through every season.

It was nice to see that something thrives here. That something can grow from death and sadness.

I wait a long moment, as if I am giving her the chance to break the silence.

I let out a long, put-upon huff. "Up to me again,

huh?" I raise an eyebrow in query,, "I really feel like I'm carrying this friendship, you know?"

The humour loosens the lump that has risen in my throat a little.

I take a swig of my now-cooled coffee and twitch my nose at the taste of lukewarm milk. Gross.

"I'm Sorry."

It is always how I start these strange little coffee dates.

Always guilty.

Always sorry.

"I missed your anniversary. Then I went and missed your birthday, too." I stare off down the path, as if I am avoiding eye contact with your ghost. "I hate running into your sister, she is always here on the big dates, and she just... I cannot even look at her without wanting to vomit, not after what she did." I rethink that, "Not after what they did... not after I saw them together, like you never existed, like she hadn't just stepped into your shoes."

I do not want the time I have with her to be about that, so I shake my head, trying to clear my thoughts of bitterness. "Nope, not today."

"Right. Well, I would ask how you have been? What you have been up to but—" I snigger at my own terrible joke. I crack myself up.

"On to me, I guess."

Where do I even start? It has been a year.

"I graduated. Finally got that Bachelor of

Business I was always yapping on about—not accounting though—Human resource management. Stop laughing."

"Ok, keep laughing. Funny Huh? Considering how much I dislike people."

"Yes, yes. I know. You're not shocked. I can practically hear you rolling your eyes."

I'm training to be a teacher now. Not primary, too much snot. Secondary – catch them as they start to become almost-adults. As critical thinking is kicking in. And I did a minor in sociology – got really into equal opportunity in education. How it could break cycles of poverty, maybe change the world. You know me, if there's a soapbox, I'm going to preach!"

"It's time to stop throwing speeches around and be the change."

Silence settles around me again. Heavy, but familiar.

I glance at her plaque.

Silent.

Until it wasn't.

I hear a shift of gravel behind me and turn, expecting to see a nondescript mourner. But I am never that lucky.

He is there. Standing on the side of the path by the row of oaks. I have not seen him in years, but his posture is the same, screaming arrogance and entitlement, hands buried in the pockets of a coat that seems too nice for a man of his character. A body bag would suit him better.

The trees cast a shadow across his face, but I can still see the smirk playing at the corner of his mouth, a smirk that feels like a challenge.

He moves toward me, and I groan inwardly.

I raise an eyebrow and tilt my head questioningly. "You lost or just sightseeing?" My voice carries a bite I hadn't used in a very long time; I'm quite pleased I can still throw that much venom into five simple words.

His smirk falters for a second. "I… I've come to pay my respects," he says, his voice careful. Testing to see if I will let it go, just accept his presence, maybe concede the space and leave.

Not likely, sunshine.

I snort, "Respect?" Then I grin like he has told me the best joke I've heard all day. "Interesting choice of words. I'm pretty sure banging her sister is the opposite of that."

The smirk finally drops away, and I look him up and down, disgust written across my face. " Oh, I get it. Thought you could come around and play the doting widower, post it up on your Facebook for a little attention and hope that everyone forgets how quickly you fell on top of the one person you shouldn't have? News flash, buddy, your narrative doesn't fly here, not now, not ever."

He opens his mouth, hesitates, "It… it wasn't like that."

I step closer, letting the air between us hum with tension.

"It was exactly like that. You didn't even wait two months before moving in with her."

He swallows and tries to stare me down. I stay, I don't flinch, I don't give him ground. He should really know better by now; this isn't our first round.

As if hearing my thoughts, he takes a hesitant step backwards, gravel shifting sharply with his sudden change of stance.

"You don't get to use her today," I say it quietly, but my words are loaded with threat.

He glances about as if someone might appear and step in to save him. Finally, he seems to remember it's just us and the dead. He spins and stomps off down the path, glancing back once to see me still rooted in place.

"Well, that was fun," I mutter to myself and force my shoulders to relax.

Returning to her plaque, I flop back onto the bench with a heavy sigh, forgetting its aversion to my volume.

"All jokes aside, I think I might have actually broken it this time."

When I don't fall through the bench, I grab up my abandoned coffee and take a long pull.

I immediately regret this life choice.

I pull a face and poke out my tongue, as if this could remove the taste of stale milk and bad decisions.

"I can hear you judging me. Maybe starting a list of reasons why I'm not allowed to buy coffee."

The breeze picks up a little, moving around me in a soft sigh. The tension he left me with eases, leaving the faintest of echoes behind.

I lean forward, elbows on my knees, and stare at her name. The glitter catches the light as it breaks through the clouds.

" You would've hated that."

"Not the yelling, you always loved a good row," I huff out a laugh, "But him. The whole situation."

My fingers trace her plaque. Soft. Careful. As if she might feel it, and the comfort I offer.

"I think that's what hurts the most," I admit softly, " That the world just kept keeping on. Without you. Like it didn't matter that you were gone or that you being gone gave them the excuse to be awful."

I swallow, my throat tight and raw.

"How could anyone just replace you … or overlap you?" I wrinkle my nose as disgust creeps back in. " You would've ripped him to shreds, your sister too."

I smile as I picture it, hands on hips. Blue eyes sparkling like ice. The look of rage before she demolished someone with her words.

"I miss that," I whisper, "that fire that made you, you."

Those words just sit there between us, heavier than anything else I've said today. No sarcasm to soften the feels. No jokes to hide behind. Just truth.

Then I laugh, a full belly laugh.

"Remember that day in the supermarket when someone pushed past that hunched old man? You tore after them, pulling them to pieces in front of a display of canned beans, loudly shaming them for their inconsideration, lack of respect … lack of care."

"When people were cruel, you always went for them."

"You were terrifying."

I let the silence stretch this time, in no rush to fill it

The wind moves through the rosemary, surrounding me with its clean, sharp scent. Familiar and grounding, and just for a moment, it doesn't feel like I'm sitting here alone.

"When you di—" I choke and try again. "When you died … I saw I had missed your sister's call at 3.19 am. I knew. I knew as I pressed call back that something terrible had happened. But there was still a shock that rattled my entire world when she said you were dead. The common cold you had that day had masked an infection in your heart. The ambulance you called for yourself was too late. You died alone, scared.

"I thought I had to let you go. That I had to move forward. That I had to say goodbye."

My mind flashes forward to your funeral. Leaning into the plywood box covered in messages written in every colour of the rainbow, pressing my lips to your face. Nothing could prepare me for how cold and hard you would be, so that it would feel like your skin was trying to steal my warmth, my life.

"And I did it, I said goodbye." The tears I've been keeping at bay make their escape and slide down my face. "You were gone. I was alone."

I sit back and look across the worn stones and clipped grass.

"I've learnt I was wrong."

"You were never gone."

"You just changed shape."

"You are in the jokes I make. In the stories I tell. In the fact that I still buy these damn flowers even when they try to kill me." I gesture to the lilies.

"You're in the glitter," I add, softly.

Another tear fights its way free, slowly tracing my cheek as if it thought it could win against gravity.

She would have appreciated the drama of it.

"I'm not going to say goodbye this time."

It would just be a lie.

"In six months or a year or ten… I will be back. With a bunch of flowers that you would have loved, and I hate."

I will bring my cold coffee, my wins and losses, my sorrow, and my joy.

I will offer a list of apologies.

I will give you my love.

And I will sit here wishing I could see you, hear you, hug you one last time.

"I miss you."

"I'll see ya soon."

On my way out of the cemetery gates, a shaft of sunlight breaks through the clouds again and reflects across the stones.

I bend down to see what could have attracted the sun's attention. There, in the rough white gravel, is a dusting of blue glitter.

I smile and feel her, as if she stands beside me.

"I love you too."

6
THE FISHERMAN AND THE BEGGAR

L. V. ELDRIDGE

Fleet learnt early that pity had a sound.

It lived in the clatter of a stale crust striking boards near his feet. It lived in laughter that came a breath after. It lived in the sigh adults made when they looked at him and decided hunger in a child was sad, though not sad enough to interrupt supper.

Kindness had a different sound. Fleet had heard it often enough to know the shape of it. He had never kept it long enough to trust it.

Evening dragged itself over the harbour in a smear of iron-grey cloud and fish blood. Wind came in off the sea sharp as a blade drawn slow. Fleet crouched under a fishmonger's stall with his tail wrapped tight to his ankle and watched silver scales tremble in the gutter light like broken coins. Men shouted over baskets. Knives knocked bone. Gulls gathered on roof-beams and mooring posts with the patient malice of thieves who knew hunger made all creatures stupid eventually.

Fleet was waiting for waste.

That was how most nights worked. Wait long enough and something fell. A strip of belly. A spine with a little flesh left on it. A fish eye if the world had woken in a cruel mood.

The fishmonger's boy tipped a pail into the runnel. Fleet moved.

So did the gulls.

White wings burst down around him. Fleet lunged, fingers closing on half a split tail before a boot thudded on the board above his head.

"Off with you, vermin."

Another kick struck the bench leg. Fleet scrambled backwards. The gulls descended in a flurry of feathers and filth, tearing apart what he had lost while the laughter above rolled after him.

He did not look back. Looking back invited stones.

He kept to the edge of the lane where the lamps failed to reach properly. The harbour climbed away from the water in a jumble of lean-tos, taverns, sail-lofts and fish sheds all warped by salt and years. Window light spilled in thin gold strips over mud. Fleet avoided staring at it. Warmth behind glass could hollow a body out from the inside.

By an old crate split through with rot, he found a strip of skin still clinging to wood. He peeled it free and swallowed it before anyone could claim offence.

"Take the wrong hand and it drags you under."

Fleet turned. Old Nara sat bundled beneath an eave in a nest of rags and sailcloth, one eye white with age, the other bright enough to cut. She had lived so long in the harbour's cracks that she seemed grown there, like mould, or spite.

Fleet wiped his mouth with the back of his hand.

Old Nara jerked her chin at him. "You hear me, gutterling?"

"Roof still better than rain," Fleet muttered.

"Aye." Her laugh sounded like dry reeds rubbing together. "Until the beams learn your name."

He left her to her muttering and went on.

He passed Hook Lane just as the tavern doors opened. Heat and light burst across the street along with the smell of ale, frying eel, wet wool and bodies packed close. Fleet slowed without meaning to. He had done that before. Hunger sometimes began in the belly and climbed until it filled the throat, the eyes, the hands.

A crust flew from inside and struck his chest.

Laughter followed.

Fleet bent for it.

Another hand reached it first.

Fleet jerked back hard enough to lose balance. The figure looming over him blocked half the doorway light. Huge shoulders. Thick arms. An oilskin coat patched more than once. Fur, silver-grey and darkened at the cuffs by old fish grease. The face above him was broad and ursan, scarred across the muzzle, one ear split at the rim. He smelled of brine, damp rope, stale spirits and the deep rank of fish left too long in a barrel.

The ursan looked down at the crust in his paw, then at Fleet.

"You hungry, little lizard?"

Fleet's gaze fixed on the bread.

The ursan crouched. "Take it."

Fleet hesitated. The feeling came at once, that small sharp tightening between his shoulders. Too close. Too easy.

The ursan's mouth twitched. "I ain't askin' twice."

Fleet snatched the crust and scuttled back.

The ursan watched him chew with the flat interest of a man watching weather. "Where d'you sleep?"

"Where I find."

The ursan grunted. "Not much to find in this cold." He thumbed uphill towards the darker edge of the harbour. "Got a hut. Got work. Nets to mend.

Fish to gut. Ye earn your keep, ye eat. Better bargain than begging at doors that hate the sight of ye."

He rose and turned away as if the offer had already been accepted.

Fleet stood with the crust in both hands, heart drumming.

From the roofline across the lane came the scrape of loose slate. Fleet glanced up. For an instant he saw a small shape crouched against the chimney-shadow: a kobold girl in an oversized brown cloak, one ear nicked, red scales turned almost black in the failing light. Then she was gone, leaving only the shifting dark and the cry of gulls.

Fleet blinked and looked back to the tavern door.

The ursan had vanished inside.

Rain began sometime after midnight.

Fleet had wedged himself beneath an overturned skiff near the breakwater, knees to chest, tail over his face. The first drops came cold. The next came harder. By dawn his rags were soaked through, and two fingers on his left hand had gone so numb he slapped them against his thigh to make sure they still belonged to him.

When the ursan found him, the sky had gone the colour of old tin.

"Well?" he asked.

Fleet looked past him to the lane, the rain, the slate roofs shedding water like contempt. He thought of Old Nara's one bright eye. He thought of freezing slowly enough to hear it happening.

The ursan held out one broad paw.

Fleet placed his small clawed hand in it.

The grip closed hard.

"Good," the ursan said.

The hut stood above the cove where the harbour gave up its pretence of order. It leaned into the cliff, black with age and salt, as though the wind had spent years trying to tear it loose and lacked patience to finish the work. Nets hung from pegs along one wall. Floats, hooks, knife sheaths and bones crowded the eaves. The place smelled of smoke, wet timber, liquor and fish oil soaked deep into the boards.

There was a stove. A table. A rope cot too short for the ursan and a pallet near the wall made from bundled sailcloth and old sacks.

"Yours," said the ursan, jerking his chin at the pallet.

Fleet stared at it.

A bowl was shoved into his hands next, tin hot enough to sting. Fish stew. Thin. Greasy. Beautiful.

Fleet drank more than ate. Salt and heat ran through him so fast it made his eyes smart.

The ursan sank onto the chair by the stove with a bottle in one paw. "Name?"

"Fleet."

"Hnh."

Fleet swallowed. "Yours?"

The ursan's gaze lifted, dark and heavy. "The one feeding ye."

After that, Fleet learnt the shape of the days.

Up before dawn. Haul water. Scrape scales from tables and floor. Mend nets until the cord cut grooves in his fingers. Carry baskets that pressed his shoulders low. Gut fish until his hands smelled of blood no matter how often he scoured them. Empty slops. Patch sails. Sweep boards. Row when told. Run when told. Keep still when told.

For a handful of days, he thought he understood the bargain.

Work. Food. Shelter. Bruises, perhaps. Shouting, certainly. Yet survivable.

The ursan, for his part, seemed made of bad weather and old resentment. Some mornings he barked instructions and nothing more. On others he drank before dusk and grew foul-tempered by the time the stove was lit. He called Fleet bait, scrap-tail, gutter-thing, hatchling, whatever amused him in the moment. Once, after Fleet mended a net cleanly, he tossed him a whole smoked sprat and laughed when Fleet caught it with both hands like a dog.

Another night, because a spoon hit the floor too loudly, he struck Fleet hard enough to set one ear ringing till dawn.

There were no rules. Only moods.

That was the first true lesson.

Fleet learnt the second when the ursan began to teach knots.

He would haul Fleet to the table after drinking and loop spare line around his wrists. "See this?" he would say, thick-fingered and smiling to himself. "No fuss. No waste. Boat work, boy. A line's honest. Does what it's told."

The line always ended tighter than the lesson required.

Fleet bore it in silence.

"Speak when I teach ye."

"Yes."

"Yes what?"

Fleet's throat worked around the old word. "Yes, sir."

The ursan would grin then, satisfied by something uglier than obedience.

Winter settled properly. The cove went dark before supper. Fleet's raw hands split at the knuckles. Salt water found every cut. The pallet remained dry most nights, and for a while Fleet made that enough. He told himself beatings could be learnt. Hunger could be measured. Men had tempers. That did not always mean murder.

The harbour itself helped him lie.

When Fleet carried baskets down to market, he

saw the world still turning as usual. Merchants argued over weight. Taverns filled. Children with full bellies ran in packs and were called indoors at dusk. Once he caught sight of the kobold girl again, the one from the roofline, slipping between barrels with a loaf tucked under one arm and a look on her face that dared the world to object. She glanced his way. No pity in it. No smile either. Only recognition, quick and sharp, before she vanished into the crowd.

Fleet told himself he had imagined that as well.

One bright morning, the sea lay calmer than hammered metal. The catch came in thick and shining. The ursan rowed back grunting with effort and satisfaction, and when they had the nets in, he slapped Fleet between the shoulders hard enough to stagger him.

"See? Worth feeding after all."

It was the nearest thing to praise Fleet had heard in the hut.

By evening the table was loaded with fish, and the ursan had opened the good bottle. One became two. His voice grew louder, his step heavier. Fleet moved carefully through the shrinking spaces of the room, hanging nets, stacking bowls, keeping his tail out from under boots.

He should have kept his eyes lowered.

Instead, when the door stood open for air, he looked out. Only for a heartbeat. Only at the last stripe of colour holding over the sea and the cliff path leading away from the hut.

"What's that face?"

Fleet stilled.

The ursan was half out of his chair, bottle in one paw, the other braced on the table. "You planning to run?"

"No."

"Liar."

The word came with startling speed. The bottle slammed onto the boards. The ursan crossed the hut in two strides, caught Fleet by the shoulder and drove him into the wall so hard the pegs above them rattled.

"You eat my food." Another shove. "Sleep by my stove." Another. "And you stand there eyeing the door like I owe ye leave?"

Fleet fought for breath. "I said no, sir."

The ursan's eyes shifted towards the hanging coils of fishing line.

Something inside Fleet went cold.

The ursan tore down a length of fine line. It flashed pale in the lamplight, thin as spider silk.

"No." The word escaped before Fleet could stop it.

The ursan laughed.

The first loop bit Fleet's throat and shocked him silent. He clawed at it, but there was nothing to grip, only that slicing pressure drawing tight beneath his jaw.

"Stop thrashing."

The ursan yanked the free end over the iron hook in the beam, the one used for hanging lanterns and wet nets. His drunken hands fumbled and cursed. He hauled again.

Pain burst bright.

Fleet kicked, heels scraping the wall. Breath vanished. The line cut deeper every time he moved. His fingers tore at it and came away scored. The lamplight smeared. The ursan's face swam huge and red before him, mouth moving around words Fleet could no longer hear.

The whole world narrowed to that line. That cruel, mean, ordinary line. Work turned weapon. Lesson turned judgement.

Fleet's lungs convulsed.

Not here.

The thought came fierce and strange through the panic. Not in this room. Not hanging like something salted for winter.

He thrashed blindly and his foot struck the table leg. The table tipped. Tin bowls crashed. The lamp skidded through spilled grease and flared.

The ursan swore and turned towards the fire.

The line slackened.

Fleet dropped. He hit the boards hard, rolled, crawled, rose half-choking and lurched for the door with one hand clamped over his throat. He did not stop until the hut was a blur behind him and the cove wind had needled tears from his eyes.

He spent that night under a jut of cliff with rain dripping down the back of his neck.

At dawn he went back.

That was the blow that went deepest.

The ursan stood by the stove, rubbing sleep from his eyes as Fleet stumbled through the door. His gaze flicked once to the bruise darkening Fleet's throat.

"Stove's out," he said. "Get it lit."

No apology. No rage worth fearing. No memory powerful enough to alter breakfast.

Fleet stared at him.

The ursan frowned. "Well? Move."

Something in Fleet gave way then. Quietly. A beam rotting from the inside.

After that, the days lost their edges.

Fleet worked. Ate when food was shoved his way. Slept when exhaustion forced him down. The bruise on his throat yellowed, then darkened again under fresh fingers when the ursan gripped him there to turn his head towards some task. He stopped looking out of the doorway. Stopped measuring weather. Stopped thinking of the harbour as a place containing roads. It became only another mouth. Another place to be seen and sorted and used.

The ursan's voice settled into him like damp.

No one wants you.

No one is coming.

Your own kind wouldn't keep you five minutes.

Fleet did not believe him at once. That would have been too simple. The lie had to be said often enough that arguing with it cost more than surrender.

The final blow came on a morning of frost.

Fleet was carrying a basket of cod down the path when his foot slipped on stone glazed white with cold. The basket went over. Fish spilled into mud and dead grass, gleaming like knives.

The ursan reached him before he was even on his knees.

The first kick caught his ribs. The second took his breath. The blows that followed blurred into weight and grunts and earth in his mouth.

"Worthless little thing," the ursan snarled. "Should've fed ye to the tide the first night."

When it was done, Fleet lay curled around himself in the mud while fish stared up with blank silver eyes. Their mouths hung open as though astonishment could survive death.

That night Fleet did not eat.

Before dawn he stood from the pallet. Every part of him ached. His throat pulled when he swallowed. The hut held its foul familiar smell. The ursan snored on the cot, one arm hanging loose, mouth open.

Fleet took nothing.

Outside, the world was the colour of ash before fire wakes. Frost silvered the cliff grass. The cove below breathed in and out against the rocks.

Fleet turned uphill.

The cliffs rose above the harbour in black shelves of stone where the wind always carried more truth than the lanes below. Folk told stories about spirits walking there. Fleet had never cared for ghost tales. The living had shown enough invention.

He climbed until the harbour shrank behind him.

When he reached the edge, dawn had not quite broken. The sea below hurled itself at the rocks with slow, patient violence.

Fleet stood with his toes at the lip and looked down.

From this height the hut was a dark crooked fleck crouched by the cove. The harbour beyond it seemed smaller than memory. Smoke lifted from chimneys. Gulls wheeled. Somewhere in those lanes Old Nara would be waking to spite the cold another day. Somewhere people would be buying fish, cursing weather, kissing children on the brow, swearing over cards, living as if the world had never once closed its hand around a throat.

The wind pulled at Fleet's ragged sleeves.

He tried to imagine the step forward.

No more waking already afraid. No more bottle

breath. No more line. No more measuring every footfall in a room too small for safety. No more hunger that taught him what his body would endure before it forgot dignity entirely.

The sea below looked brutal. Honest too.

Fleet closed his eyes.

"You'll miss the clean drop."

The voice behind him was young, rough-edged, and entirely unafraid.

Fleet spun.

The kobold girl from the harbour stood a little way down the path. Brown cloak. Nicked ear. Soot-dark red scales. She was smaller than he had remembered. Harder too. In one hand she held a cloth bundle.

Fleet's heart lurched with anger so quick it nearly felt like relief. "Go away."

"No."

"No?"

She shrugged. "No."

Fleet stared at her. "Why are you here?"

"I saw you leave the cove."

"So?"

"So people climb here for one of two reasons. To watch storms or to end something. You didn't bring a coat."

It was such a dry answer that a broken laugh almost escaped him. He bit it back.

The girl stepped closer, then sat on a flat stone

still well clear of the edge. She unwrapped the cloth bundle enough for the smell to reach him.

Bread.

Smoked fish.

Fleet hated his body for turning towards it. Hated the hot rush of need that made his hands shake.

The girl tore the loaf in two. She ate a piece herself first. Then she held the other half out.

Fleet did not move.

"You got a name?" she asked.

The question struck harder than pity ever had.

Down in the hut, his name had thinned to something useful only for orders. Up here, with the sea waiting beneath him, it returned all at once, heavy and tender and his.

"Fleet," he said hoarsely.

The girl nodded. "Mara."

She kept her hand out.

Fleet stared at it.

The fisherman's hands had always been made for closing. Grips. Fists. Knots. A paw at the back of his neck. Fingers biting shoulder or throat. Every touch had meant keep, drag, punish, own.

Mara's hand did none of those things.

It simply waited.

The sea pounded below them. The harbour still existed. The hut still existed. Whatever came after this cliff would be cold and hard and uncertain.

Bread would run out. Roads would stay long. Pain would not loosen its grip merely because dawn had found him alive.

Yet the lie had cracked.

There was something else in the world.

Fleet stepped back from the edge.

His knees nearly folded under him. Mara did not rush to catch him. She only rose when he reached her and pressed the bread into his trembling hand.

He devoured it with humiliating speed. Mara looked away and gave him that small scrap of dignity on purpose. When he finished, she passed him the fish.

The salt and smoke hit his empty belly so hard it hurt.

"Why?" he asked when he could speak again.

Mara weighed the word. "Because someone should have done it for me once."

Fleet looked at her properly then.

Bruises lingered in the yellow-green shadows beneath one side of her jaw. Her cloak had been mended badly in three places, with the sort of stitches made in haste or by shaking hands. Her mouth held itself in a hard line that belonged to people who had learnt the cost of soft faces.

She knew the look.

Fleet lowered his eyes.

Mara held out her hand again.

This time there was no bread in it. No trade. No demand.

Only a choice.

Fleet thought of the hut crouched below like a rotten tooth in the cliffside. He thought of the fisherman waking to an empty pallet and cursing only the lost labour. He thought of Old Nara saying the wrong hand drags you under.

Slowly, as if his arm belonged to some other, braver creature first, Fleet placed his hand in Mara's.

Her grip closed warm and firm, no tighter than it needed to.

It nearly undid him.

"Where?" he whispered.

Mara glanced east, where dawn was beginning at last to thin the horizon. "Away first."

It was not much of an answer.

It was enough.

Together they turned from the cliff.

The path wound along black stone glazed white with frost. Below them the sea kept throwing itself against the rocks, ancient and indifferent. Behind them, the cove and hut shrank with every step. Fleet did not look back.

His throat still hurt. His ribs ached. Hunger would come again. Fear would walk beside him for a while yet, perhaps longer than that. He knew enough of life to know a single kindness did not mend what had been broken.

Still, Mara's hand remained in his.

For the first time in longer than he could remember, Fleet was moving towards something he had chosen.

By the time the sun lifted pale over the water, the harbour lay behind them, and the day, harsh though it would be, belonged to the living.

7

YA YA

L. LESTRANGE

abuse, assault, violence, and themes of survival.

Please read with care.

I learned early that silence is a currency.

You spend it to survive. You spend it when the questions come too fast. When the hands come too close. When the door locks behind you and the world shrinks into a room that smells like sweat and something metallic you don't want to name. You spend it because screaming doesn't change anything. It just makes them laugh.

Evan used to kiss me as if I mattered.

That's the part that still hurts. Not what he turned into. Not what he allowed to happen. Not even what he did. He used to look at me like I was his everything, as if he would burn the world down for me. Like I was something fragile that could easily break. Like he cared if I did break.

He doesn't look at me like that anymore.

The first time he asked, still loops in my mind. "They just want to meet you," he said, pacing the apartment as if something was chewing through his bones from the inside. "Just hang out. Talk. That's it."

I remember I laughed. Not because it was funny, but because somehow I already knew. "You're lying."

"I'm not—"

"You are. You are not telling me everything. You expect me to believe they are going to pay just to talk to me?"

His jaw ticked. His eyes darted anywhere but at me.

"They'll pay," he said finally. "Just once. We need it."

We always needed it—for rent, for food, for his debts. He never explained what he was in debt for; he just made it sound like it would be terrible if we didn't get the money. I asked him why we couldn't just get jobs. That conversation? Never ended well.

"I don't want to," I countered, and for a second—just a mere second—I thought that might count. Then he got quiet, his body tense like a storm about to unfold.

"I'm not asking."

That was the moment something inside me folded in on itself. Not broken yet, just bent.

The first time, I told myself it would also be the last. That's the trick, right? You build yourself a lie small enough to swallow. *Just this once. Just tonight. Just survive this.*

After that, the nights bled into each other, turning into gloomy memories.

It didn't matter anymore where it happened or who was in the room. Every single time it ended the same: locked doors, a similar smell clinging to everything, me staring at the ceiling, counting insults and breaths just to survive one last time. But the actual *last time* never came.

Evan always waited outside. That was his line. Was how he justified it. He didn't come in. He didn't touch me. He just handed me over like I was something he could rent out and still call his own.

Sometimes he cried afterward. Never during. Like holding it in until it was over, made him better somehow. Like that was supposed to mean something.

"I'm sorry," he'd whisper, pressing his forehead to mine. "I'm so sorry. Just a little longer. I swear."

I stopped answering him eventually because there was nothing left to say.

I thought about leaving a few times. The one time I tried, he beat the hell out of me, which caused more issues because I had to miss a few set-ups.

Something about tonight felt off. I could feel it the second we pulled up in front of the building.

This structure was bigger. Too clean in the way expensive places are—exuding the air that nothing out of the ordinary could happen there because everything is too lavish. That's how they hide it. That's how they make it feel normal.

Evan didn't meet my eyes when he opened the car door.

"Just … do what they say," he muttered.

My fingers tightened in my lap. "Evan—"

"Please," he snapped, too promptly. Too obvious. Then softer, sweeter at the edges. "Please don't make this harder," as if I were the problem.

I almost ran. God, I almost did. My body even leaned back, as if it knew and begged me to save it.

But then I saw his hands shaking again, and I remembered the threats. The ones whispered late at night. The ones about what would happen if he didn't pay. What could happen to both of us.

I got out of the car, a strange weight twisting in my chest the second my feet touched the pavement. Something about the building felt wrong, as if the air itself was whispering to me to leave, but I ignored it. I always ignored it. I pushed the door closed behind me and stepped forward.

The elevator ride didn't feel elevating at all, but more like sinking. Floor numbers climbed while something inside me dropped lower and lower. The reflection in the mirrored wall didn't look like me. Just a girl wearing my face. Eyes vacant. Soul already gone.

The door opened, and I walked in. There were six men there, all in suits, laughing and having what appeared to be a great time. I smelled the booze all over them. The older one in the middle—the one you could tell was in charge—raised his hand and beckoned me over with just one curled finger.

"Well, look at this," one of them said, leaning back in his chair. "Evan didn't oversell."

"Yeah," another laughed. "Didn't think he had the balls to actually share her."

"He didn't," a third voice chimed in. "He's desperate. Gambling'll do that to you."

A few of them laughed at that.

"How much does he owe now?" someone asked.

"Enough to make her worth it," the older one said, his eyes still on me. "That's all that matters."

"She know what she's here for?" another one joined in.

"Does it matter?" Another scorned before taking a sip from his drink.

"Probably told her some bullshit," the one at the far end of the table added. "They always do."

More laughter echoed around the room.

I walked over to him, and he leaned forward, putting his hand up my dress. I cringed a little. He did not like that.

"Oh, look, boys! We have some fucking bitch who thinks she's too good for us."

The punch came fast. Unexpected. I swear I saw stars dancing in front of me.

They all began laughing, taking turns punching and biting me. Not sure which one pulled my hands so violently behind my back, I heard my shoulder crack as it popped out of its socket. Another grabbed an electrical cord and tied my hands up, then pushed me over the edge of a chair.

Then came the ... *cutter*. He pulled out a knife

and shredded my clothes, recklessly, also slicing through my skin. It stung like a thousand paper cuts all over my body.

One touched between my legs and laughed, "Oh, look, boys! This bitch really thinks she is too good for us. She's not even wet. Dry like the Sahara Desert."

"We should play rock, paper, scissors for the first turn," another shouted.

I have never felt pain like this before.

Then one rammed me in my ass with no lube. Pain ripped through me, and I screamed. That didn't slow them down but seemed only to further arouse them. My eyes swelled shut, and I couldn't see anything anymore. All my senses numbed. I only heard cheering and encouragement.

"Oh, look, boys! That ass is bleeding. Let's find out how much further it can bleed."

My mind went dark. I am not sure when or how, but when I came to, I was sitting on one guy while another fucked me in my ass. Someone tilted my head up. I couldn't make a face. But he said, "Bite my dick, bitch, and I will fucking kill you. Open wide."

I did as I was told. He slammed into my mouth so forcefully that I vomited all over his dick. Another punch shattered my face, and that was the last thing I remembered.

When I opened my eyes again, nothing made

sense at first. The room was still there, but it felt different, like time had moved without me. I didn't know how long I'd been out, and I didn't know what had happened while I was gone.

When I came to, it wasn't all at once. The room returned in pieces. Slow and rather distorted, like something had continued while I wasn't there to feel it. My body ached in ways I didn't understand. Deep, as if someone had done something to me, and I couldn't remember.

There's always a moment after, when everything goes quiet—too quiet—like the world forgot you existed. Time doesn't move the same there, stretching and bending, as you try to crawl back into your own body and remember how to breathe.

Something sticky pressed against my cheek, and it took me a second to realize it was my blood. The metallic smell filled my lungs every time I tried to take a deeper breath. I forced myself into smaller, shallower breaths. Anything that felt safe. Anything that didn't make it worse.

Somewhere in the distance, a thought surfaced. Loud.

Get up.

It wasn't deafening or urgent. Just there, steady and impossible to ignore, repeating itself until it felt like the only thing keeping me anchored.

Get up.

My fingers twitched, and pain invaded

everywhere. It wasn't sharp or clean, but heavy and completely shattering. My body no longer felt like mine. It felt used up and left behind.

Get up.

I slowly rolled onto my side, the room spinning as black spots crawled into my vision, and for a second I thought I was going to pass out again. Part of me wanted to sink back into it and disappear, but something colder pushed through the fog: a quiet certainty that pierced through everything else.

If you stay here, you will die.

That did it.

I pushed myself up slowly, my body spasming with every movement that triggered something broken. And that was when it hit me: I was naked, the cold pressing into my skin, settling deep into me as everything came back. Too real. Too invasive. When I forced myself to look up, I saw a man's jacket hanging on the door. Left behind without care, as if it hadn't been worth taking.

Something soft and out of place brushed against my side as I shifted. I stilled, and my gaze dropped, my mind struggling to understand why it was there.

Slowly, carefully, as if it might slip away if I moved too fast, I reached for it. Peeled it from my skin, my fingers shaking as I held it in front of me, trying to focus through the narrow slits of my swollen eyes. It was just a card. Simple, but the message on it didn't feel simple at all.

666 Wonderland Way
Floor 4, Apt. 7
Ask for Madeline

My throat tightened, and I read it again, as if it might carry a different message. As if I had misunderstood it the first time. I lifted my head and looked around the room. Really looking this time, my eyes scanning every corner, every shadow. Searching for any sign that someone had been there, that someone might still watch me.

But there was nothing. Only a heavy, suffocating silence that fell over everything, so complete it felt as if life itself had dismissed me.

The door wasn't locked. It never was after. Not because they think you won't leave, but because they expect you to, like taking out the trash. The hallway was empty, bright—too bright—fluorescent lights buzzing overhead as I dragged myself to the elevator. I pressed the button and waited.

Every second ticked like a countdown, as if someone could step out, grab me, drag me back, and finish what they started. When the doors finally opened, I stumbled inside and hit the first-floor button. The mirror caught me again, but this time I didn't look.

When the doors opened, I walked. Didn't run, because walking was quieter, safer, and less noticeable. The night air hit me like a slap—cold, real, biting, and I nearly collapsed right there, on the sidewalk. Then I saw the car.

Evan was still there, leaning against the hood, smoking as if nothing had happened. Like this was just another ordinary night.

He looked up at me, relief flickering across his face as he started toward me. "Hey," he said, already reaching, acting like everything was fine. "What the hell took you so long? You're—" I didn't stop. "Hey, wait. What? " he called after me, his voice shifting as I walked right past him without looking, without slowing down. "Where are you going?" he shouted, panic creeping into his voice, now louder, aggressive, like he was losing control of something he thought he owned.

Good. Let him panic for once. Let him feel even a fraction of what I had been feeling this whole time. And I kept trudging, no idea whatsoever where I was headed, or where that strength came over me.

"Leave me alone," I barely mumbled through swollen lips, and I couldn't even raise my arm to give him the finger.

"Get in the car," his voice boomed, as if the change in tone would fix everything. "We need to go."

We? Are you fucking kidding me? There is no we.

I almost laughed, but no sound came out. Instead, I kept walking, barefoot, bleeding, as if trying to leave him behind, or at least put distance between us. Even only a few feet would do right now.

"Don't do this," he snapped, moving faster now, almost charging, the space between us dangerously dissolving.

I didn't answer. I couldn't even open my mouth, and honestly? I wasn't sure what would come out if I did.

Evan caught up with me and yanked my hair, pulling me back toward him with so much force that my body jerked with it. I thought he would apologize after what happened. Thought maybe this was the moment he would finally see it. He'd finally see me. But no, he just slapped me across the face.

"Listen, bitch! Never walk away from me again."

Before I could react, before I could fight it, he grabbed me and picked me up, then shoved me into the car.

A few days passed after that night, though it didn't feel like time so much as something I was floating through. I stayed in bed most of it, lights dim, curtains barely open, my body aching in ways I didn't want to think about. Every movement triggered in me something I couldn't fully recollect. Something my mind kept just out of reach. And I stopped trying to chase it because I thought it was better if I didn't remember.

Evan didn't give me that same courtesy. Initially, anger surfaced. Not vocal, not explosive, definitely not immediate. But clear in his cutting words, his movements around the apartment, and his glare that judged my mere existence.

One afternoon, he paced back and forth as if he were the one trying to recover, and said, "Do you have any idea how bad it is? I had to reschedule two nights because you look like shit."

I didn't answer because there wasn't anything left to say.

The next day, he was different. Gentler. He brought me food I didn't touch and sat on the edge of the bed like he used to. Like the version of him I kept trying to hold on to was still there, somewhere. His hand hovered over my arm before finally resting there, light and careful. Almost protective.

"I'm so sorry. Seeing you like this, it hurts," Evan said, crying.

He almost fooled me. But by now, I knew. Fake tears. He didn't care at all. Not about me, anyway.

I closed my eyes and let him talk, his voice low and steady. Almost comforting if you didn't listen too closely. And when he finally left, the quiet descended again, peaceful and oddly familiar. I pushed my hand under the pillow and felt the card right where I had put it.

One day, cold and ruthless; the next, he'd act as if nothing had happened, or as if he were sorry.

Then one morning, he seemed to be back to normal, or at least his version of normal. He moved around the apartment as if the last few days had been a pause instead of a warning. And when he leaned against the doorway that afternoon, watching me from across the room, something stilled in his expression, making my stomach turn.

"Tomorrow," he said casually, as if he were talking about dinner. "I set something up. Better place. Better money."

The words settled firm and final. Not a question. Not a suggestion. A decision he had already made. Not for himself, but for me.

"No," I said, the word slipping out before I could stop it.

Then it was silence, barely there, but it was the first real thing I had said in days, and it was enough to make him go still. "What?" he asked, like he hadn't heard me right, but I didn't repeat it because I didn't feel I needed to.

Instead, I just said, "You heard me."

The air in the room shifted as he pushed himself off the doorframe and stepped closer, his voice dropping to a low and controlled tone. Sounding almost humble. And that felt worse than yelling. "Don't start that again. We've already been through this," he said.

I didn't look at him. My fingers tightened around the edge of the blanket, grounding myself in something real, something that still felt like mine. "I said no."

The silence that followed thickened between us, heavier than anything he had said before, and for a second I thought he might explode. But he did something unexpected. He laughed, short and senseless, a sound void of significance.

"That was never an option," he said, as if it were a statement, not an ultimatum. "Be ready," he barked, already turning away, done with the conversation. "Tomorrow night. And you don't get to say no."

The door closed behind him, and for the first time, I believed him. Even worse, I knew exactly what would come if I stayed. I lay there for a long time after he left, staring at the ceiling as the stillness enveloped me again.

Something in me stirred. Not wild or dramatic, just clear in a way nothing else had been. I thought about the card, about the address, about the way it had felt in my hand, like something left behind for only me.

Slowly, I reached over to the nightstand and picked up the card.

666 Wonderland Way. Floor 4. Apartment 7. Ask for Madeline.

My fingers trembled as the word *tomorrow* echoed in my head, over and over again, until it didn't feel like panic anymore. It felt like determination.

He thought I would be ready. He was right.

I was ready. Just not for what he expected.

I didn't move right away, but sat there with the card in my hand, turning it over between my fingers, afraid it might vanish if I looked away. As if something this small and simple couldn't possibly be real. But it was, and the longer I stared at it, the clearer everything else became. Not immediately. Not abrupt and final, but just a logical understanding creeping in.

If I stayed, nothing would change, and tomorrow would come as it always did. Him taking me somewhere new, somewhere worse, maybe. Me, surviving the same way I always had—fading away until there was nothing left of me to come back to.

I couldn't do that again, and I wouldn't.

The decision didn't feel like power or bravery. It felt suppressed, but decisive.

Patiently, I waited until later that night. Until the apartment settled into that familiar routine. Until he ceased watching me so closely, and I began moving through the dark, cautious, careful not to rattle something, but with the confidence of someone who had already decided.

When he asked for food, I nodded and ambled into the kitchen, keeping my head down, every sluggish step reminding me how little of it I could actually control. My arm wouldn't bend properly, still hanging heavy and useless at my side. That night, something had rearranged and never settled back into place. Each uncalculated movement sent a dull ache shooting through my shoulder. I worked around it the best I could, using my other hand and keeping everything simple. I kept tasks to a minimum, taking on only those that required little strength or precision.

THE BOTTLE WAS EXACTLY where I had left it. I stared at it for longer than I meant to, my fingers fiddling before I finally picked it up. I fished out one pill. Then another. Meticulously, I crushed them and mixed everything without thinking too much, because thinking would have made me stop. And I had no intention of stopping. Not now.

I carried the plate out to him and set it down without meeting his eyes. My pulse steadied in a way that didn't feel real, and it felt like watching myself from above. He didn't question or notice anything, but just ate as he always did. Distant. Already half-focused on something else, something that, of course, didn't include me. The same detachment I refused to believe in for so long. I suppressed a smirk. *Nothing new.*

My fingers curled into fists, and my eyebrows pinched as I looked at the man I thought was my everything, realizing how wrong I was.

But today? Today, that will change.

I waited with a patience I didn't recognize as my own, and it didn't take long before his words slowed and his movements lagged just enough to show. When he finally leaned back, eyelids heavy, and blinked as if he were trying to stay awake, I knew it. It was time.

"Go to bed," I whispered, the words slipping out more comforting than I anticipated, and he barely argued.

By the time he made it to the bedroom, he was already halfway gone. Without another word, he collapsed cold onto the mattress, breathing peacefully even. My stomach squeezed. Not out of guilt, not really. It was simply recognition. He had never looked so tranquil. Not even when I needed him to be.

I stood there for a moment, watching him, making sure. Waiting for any sign that he might wake up or that my plan might fall apart at the last second. But he didn't move, and that was somewhat reassuring.

I turned away and shuffled back to the other room, my movements careful as I pulled out a bag and started packing. I took a little. Only what I needed. Whatever much I could manage with one working arm: a pair of pants, a soft, oversized sweater, enough to cover me without hurting, underwear, shoes. I moved stealthily, adjusting and ignoring the way my body protested every single time I reached too far or bent the wrong way.

The card went in last, on top of everything else.

I zipped the bag with shaky fingers and paused for a second as the eerie silence took over the space for the last time. Heavier now, as if the apartment itself was holding its breath. I didn't look back at the bedroom because I knew that if I gave myself even a second to hesitate, I probably wouldn't leave.

Deep down, I knew it. It wasn't the right time for second thoughts. I was done. Determination pushed me forward.

I stood by the door longer than I should have, my hand resting on the handle. Listening to nothing but the silence behind me and the hefty weight of everything waiting ahead. The bag hung heavy on my shoulder, the other arm still hanging useless at my side. For a second, I thought about sitting back down, maybe waiting until morning, at least. Thought about pretending I had more time than I actually had. The fear of the unknown began creeping in, settling deeper the longer I stood there.

But I didn't cave under my own fears. I knew exactly what morning meant.

I took a deep breath, opened the door, and bravely stepped out into the night.

Colder than I had expected.

The air bit into my skin immediately, slipping under the sweater, sneaking into places that already hurt. The street greeted me, deserted, and the late-night quiet made everything feel too motionless, as if the world stood still. I pulled the sweater tighter around me and started walking. Slowly at first, hesitant, my body crippled and uncooperative.

It didn't take long for the pain to catch up.

Every step pulled at something sore, something faulty. My shoulder ached with every slight motion, and my legs jellied, weaker than I wished them to be. I had to stop more than once, leaning against whatever I could find—walls, fences, anything sturdy—just to steady a little before forcing myself forward again.

The place wasn't far, but it felt like it. Although I wasn't really sure how far it was. All I knew was that with every step, it felt like chasing an illusion impossible to reach.

Everything felt much farther at one in the morning, when the streets stretched longer, and the silence pressed heavier. When every shadow looked like it might come to life, and every passing car made my chest burn.

I thought about turning back more than once. And just as many times, I almost did.

But every instance I slowed down, every time I hesitated, *tomorrow* flashed in my head—clear and undeniable—and that prospect alone pushed me forward again.

One step. Then another. And another.

By the time I found the building, I was nearly out of breath and shuddering from the depths of my core.

Not just from the cold, but from everything else: exhaustion, ache, fear. All blended together until I felt like I might collapse before I even made it inside. The building looked smaller than I expected. Older, not dilapidated, but worn out in a way that made it easy to miss if you weren't looking for it.

Perfect. I made it.

I climbed the stairs slowly, my good hand gripping the railing, pulling myself up one step at a time, breath uneven, vision hazy. By the time I reached the fourth floor, my legs felt like they might give out under me completely.

Apartment 7

I stood there for a second, staring at the door, hand clenched on the card, my heart pounding harder now than it had been the entire walk.

I swallowed and knocked, then waited, and it seemed longer than it probably was.

Long enough for doubt to tiptoe in, for my mind to start turning against me, whispering that this was a mistake. That no one would answer, and I had come all this way for nothing.

Then the lock clicked. The door opened with a slow squeak.

She stood there, framed in the doorway, looking at me like she had already seen everything I had been through without me saying a word.

"Yes?" she said, her voice calm and plain. "How can I help you?"

I tried to speak, but nothing came out at first. My throat felt too strained, my body too weary, and when I finally lifted my head enough to look at her properly, something in my chest twisted.

There was sadness on her face. Not restraint, nor pity.

Something profound. Something that looked like understanding.

"I…" My voice cracked. "I'm looking for Madeline."

For a second, she just stared; didn't answer.

Then something flipped in her expression, small but unmistakable.

"What can I help you with?" she asked.

My fingertips turned white, clutching the card

as I turned it over. My vision blurred again as I tried to focus on its back.

The words were simple: ya ya.

"I—" My voice wavered. " ya ya."

I held it out to her.

She looked at it. Then at me. And then …

A voice, pitched and bright and completely out of place, cut through the quiet. "Oh, I guess it's time for a new monologue," Alice said.

TO LEARN MORE ABOUT MADELINE, check out Acidic Honey

8
HEALING WOUNDS

TIM GRAYSON

Beneath a roof that whispered fear,
A child learned to hide, to disappear.
Shadows stretched long across the floor,
Each footstep echoing threats once more.
He folded small, he held his tears,
counted the nights, endured the years.
The world was heavy, cold, unkind,
but something flickered deep in mind.
A quiet spark, a stubborn light,
that whispered softly through the night:
You are more than what they've done.
You will rise; you will see the sun.
And one day, the walls grew thin,
The storm passed, and he breathed within.
Step by step, he claimed the sky,
scared but strong, he learned to fly.
Now he blooms where darkness fell
a story of survival he alone can tell.

9

QUAIL AND THE TECHNICOLOR WINDOW PANE

M. T. SOMMER

For reasons that were wildly out of my control, I found myself stuck in an endless loop of February mourning. Though there was no loss to speak of, each day brought the same sensation of expecting one more step on the stairs. The jarring confusion of my foot landing heavy and late, and the unfairness of reality not aligning with what my body believed to be true.

And each morning that misstep would shake loose the parts of me that were barely clinging on. Because depression, at least for me, was all about the weight of things. My limbs were too heavy. My thoughts were heavier still. Even the colours carried so much weight that they slipped and dripped and bled from the air until the whole world was washed in white like a sun-bleached photograph of somebody else's life. Someone who felt all the things that were now laid to rest on the floor where they fell.

The version of me who was standing at the window? She didn't care that the ground around her was littered with cast off pieces. Tripping over memories only hurt when they were coloured in, after all. But it was on that morning, at that window when everything changed.

I wish it had been something significant so I wouldn't have to search for validation in being stuck in the dark for so long in the first place. Or something replicable so that I could brag about my infallible three-step system that is guaranteed to work on any morning at every window.

There was no grand measure of grace or infomercial-style intervention.

There were just quail.

Of all the birds it could have been… A murder of crows; an unkindness of ravens—I'd even have taken a wake of vultures.

NOPE. I got a covey of quail.

Flitting around each other as if their choreography was fuelled by caffeine and telepathy, they pecked uselessly at my bare lawn. While it had been a mild winter, I had never been the gardening type, so there was barely grass, let alone seeds or bugs. More importantly, I hadn't ever seen them in my yard before.

So why now?

Why migrate to my patchy plot of barren land?

Why show up when all I wanted was to be left alone?

I wished, not for the first time, that my dog was still with me. I would have let him out to chase the birds away. And then immediately felt weird about myself. Because of all the reasons to wish him back to life, this was just sheer pettiness. I'd always had some curmudgeonly tendencies, but this was a new level.

Which was sort of embarrassing, and also funny in that way that no one laughs at when you try to explain it. There's just no punchline to the whole "how dare my dog be dead when there is a freaking covey of quail attacking my yard" bit. But it was funny.

I could see it play out in my mind—from my dog's ears flopping with each bounding stride as he chased the birds from the yard to the sound of forty wings fluttering in a panicked whoosh as they took to the sky. That's what birds do when something scares them. They fly away. And it was in that moment that a very tragic epiphany threaded its way around my ribs and cinched me up too tight to breathe. I realized that if I was a member of that covey, staring down the snout of a charging black hell beast, I would stand my ground. Not because I was brave or stupid—though some may argue they're synonymous in situations such as those.

No, I wouldn't have flown off because somewhere along the line, that instinct to protect myself got too heavy and fell away from me. That voice in the back of my head had gone quiet from screaming uselessly for so long. I had been the void into which she was wailing, and her words were all eaten by the silence inside me.

So when I should have left, I stayed.

When I should have run, I waited.

And when I should have fought back, I took the hit instead.

It was still just a covey of quail in a winter-deadened yard, but the window between us was painted with my reflection, and I could see something different in my eyes. Echos and impressions of memories that could have changed the course of my entire life, had I just been able to hear her. Had I been strong enough to carry her?

But I didn't listen.

And I only had enough strength to survive, so I had let her go.

Staring at the glass, crying as I watched the ways I could have done so much better by myself, I realized that Eminem was right. There's a reason why it's called a window pane.

Pain, though, isn't a bad thing. Like fear, pain is necessary for survival. And despite all evidence to the contrary, I did want to survive. So I embraced it.

It had been a long mourning, stuck stilted at apathy, and everything after that burned. I had gone from nothing to annoyance, then shame, and onto humour all so swiftly that they hadn't seemed real. But the hurt… That I felt.

And I revelled in it.

It spread like it already knew the course of my veins, and each infected limb pulsed slowly back to life.

I wasn't suddenly better. The world wasn't suddenly technicolour like I fell out of Kansas and landed in Oz, but the veil between me and my emotions had thinned.

It was a step forward, small but measurable, and that's what mattered. More often than not, it's those singular moments that make the difference. They aren't loud or doused in glitter. It's not a grand gesture or inspirational speech.

It's standing at a window, feeling nothing, until you suddenly do.

That day didn't just help me find a way out of my depressive episode. It also gave me back the voice that had only wanted to keep me safe. Just a whisper at first, scratchy from neglect, and quick to fade if ignored. But there she was all the same. And every time I listened, she got a little louder. Every time she was right, I trusted her a little bit more.

I wouldn't say that this is a particularly strong skill of mine, nor do I expect to win a medal at intuitive listening. I'm still proud of it, though. I have bigger, better accomplishments, but this one? This one matters. This one was won back inch by inch, pound by pound, through shades of grey as they saturated to sepia and then burst into a vibrant kaleidoscope of bright colours.

There were false alarms, tears, and shame, all shadowed by guilt and frustration at every failure. There was disbelief when I got it right, and anger that it had been as simple as just listening. It was too easy. It felt like a trap.

That self doubt led to long days, longer nights, and an unsettled quiet that I didn't feel like I could trust. But then there were moments when I found myself resting in the silence, realizing that when the alarm actually works, you don't have to show constant vigilance. When you can tell the difference between safety and threats, you start remembering how to accept the peace when it's presented to you.

They say that grace is the measure of the fall, so maybe I still have a ways to go before I've done all the work it takes to deserve it, but I'm not waiting to forgive myself for the things I had to lose to survive. The woman I was before wasn't perfect, but she got me to that window on that February morning.

Every day since has been about movement. Sometimes it's a few feet, sometimes just a couple of inches, but it's always forward. I know this because even if I slip back a step, that doesn't restart the count to zero.

If I walk a hundred paces ahead and give three

up, I'm still ninety-seven steps further than where I was when I started.

Small steps matter.

Small moments matter.

And, sometimes, the most important epiphanies of your life will begin with something as small as a covey of quail.

10

GOOD NIGHT SIS

WHEN I LOST MY SOUL

BELLADONNA

Graphic, on-page content around child sexual abuse. Written from the victim's perspective. Proceed with caution.

- Good night, sis.

- Good night, Amalia. Try to sleep now.

- Okay, I will try. But the music is too loud, and it's hard to shut the noise out. Do you think they will turn it down soon?

- Amalia... sleep now. Just close your eyes and relax, and you will fall asleep.

- Sis?

- Yes.

- Thank you for letting me sleep in your room.

I don't like to sleep in my room; it's too dark, and I don't like the dark. But I have Wolfie, my stuffed toy, and he is my best friend. I never sleep without him. My sister got him for me a year ago when I was turning 3. I'm a big girl now, my mom says, and can sleep without him and in my own room. My sister is four years older than I am, and I think she is so cool and awesome. She always pities me and lets me sleep in her room. She has a two-seater couch that she lets me sleep on. I'm so small that the couch feels like a king-size bed for me.

Mom and Dad invited their friends today for a party, and I really like it when we have people home, because they always play with me, and I love to play around and make people laugh.

- Amalia, are you even trying to sleep? Because I can hear you humming.

- Sorry, sis… I will close my eyes now. Love you. Good night.

- Good night, Amalia

I finally start to fall asleep when I see a big shadow in the opening of the door, but I don't say anything. What if it is a monster from my room that has come to look for me?

The big shadow steps into the room and moves closer to the couch where I'm sleeping and sits down beside me. I scootch in so he can sit.

- Hi, Amalia. Are you sleeping?

I know that voice. It's one of my mom's friends, and he is so nice and has been joking around with me almost all day, and I really like him.

- I try. My sister says that I have to sleep, but the music is too loud, so it's hard.

- Oh, I understand, Amalia. The music will stop soon, everyone is going home in a minute, and then you can sleep.

- Thank you, my eyes are tired, and I have a problem with keeping them open.

- Don't you sleep with a pajamas, Amalia?

- No, I don't like that. It moves around and makes me warm.

- Ohh, your panties are cute. Is it butterflies on them?

- Yes, my mom got them for me. I like butterflies; they are so beautiful and free.

He takes his hand and touches my panties, but my mom told me once that no one can touch me there.

- No! My mom says that no one is allowed to touch them.

- But you are so cute and sweet, and I just want to feel the fabric.

He takes his hand and lifts my panties, and I try to get his hand away, but he is too strong. And he just keeps smiling at me. I don't understand why he isn't listening to me when I don't want him touching me there. What will my mom say when I tell her?

She is going to be so mad at me for letting him touch me this way, because she has told me so many times that no one can touch me there. Will she believe me when I tell her that I really tried to push him away?

- Oh, look at this… You don't have a single hair here, so I can see everything.

- No… Stop! Don't do this! I will tell Mom if you don't stop!

- Shhh… I'm just looking. And you have been so cute all day with that dress, and your laugh is magical.

I can feel him putting his fingers at the edge of my panty line, just inside of my thigh. I start to wiggle up on the couch, but I'm stuck and have nowhere to move. I can feel my eyes watering, and I just think about everything my mom ever said, and I can't understand why he is doing this.

He was so nice earlier, but now he acts like the monster

that is hiding under my bed, and this monster is just smiling at me like this is nothing.

- Please stop… I don't want to. Please, no. Please.

His hand just moves closer to my apex, and I close my eyes and let my tears fall in hope that this is just a nightmare, and I will wake up soon. But as my tears fall, he doesn't stop. He moves closer to my slit, and I wiggle more so it will be harder for him to reach, but he is strong…so strong.

And I grip his wrist and use all the strength that I have to make him understand.

His other hand grips my leg and holds it still, making me feel more trapped, and my tears fall faster, making my vision blurry. All of a sudden I feel pain, and I realize that he has a finger inside me, and the pain is making my stomach turn, but I try to stay quiet so my mom doesn't get mad at me for not being strong enough to stop this. I know that this isn't right, but no one has ever shown me how I'm supposed to end it.

- Amalia, you're a really sweet girl… and I like how you feel around my finger, so wet and tight. I would love to feel more of that sweet little pussy of yours around something more than just my finger. Would you like that, Amalia?

I try to move my body and kick with my leg, but it is in vain. He is to strong and I can't shake him of me. I close my eyes harder and try to think about something fun, like that time me and my friend, that lives just next door to us, was playing up on the ruin that is a old barn that burned down many years before.

It's the perfect playground for us; it's close to home, so our parents can just call us in when it's time to eat. We play horses most of the time when we play, and it's so easy to lose track of time. I really love to play with her. We live out on the countryside so there is not many children her for me to play with.

- Who are you? What the fuck are you doing here?

I hear my sister's voice screaming out loud, and his finger pulls out quickly and he gets to his feet.

- Oh, I was just on my way to the bathroom, and I just checked in to see that everyone was okay.

- Yeah? Get away from my sister, you're not supposed to be in here.

He starts to walk towards the door and laughs, closing the door behind him.

The monster is gone, but my tears won't stop to fall from my eyes, and I really just want my mom here to hold me. The music stops and I can hear cars starting outside the house. My sister rushes up from her bed and sits down beside me, asking me what he wanted and if he did something. So I tell her what happened and I hide my face in my palms, the feeling rushing over me as soon as she says that he is not allowed to touch you the way he did, and that we can't talk to mother tonight because she is drinking.

- We will tell mom in the morning, Amalia, and mom is going to be so angry.

- You promise? I'm scared to tell mom, she is going to be so angry with me for not being strong enough.

- She is not going to be mad, Amalia... This is not your fault. If you want, you can sleep in my bed with me the rest of the night.

She smiles at me with warmth, and I feel like she is my hero, just like Super Ted.

I take my pillow and slowly rise from the couch, my whole body feels weak and my stomach hurts from crying and struggling so long. My chest is heavy and it feels like a vein burst from my heart. Why did he do that? He was my friend. Are all adults like this? I don't understand why someone would do something like this. Was my voice not loud enough?

I walk across the room towards my sister's bed, with my pillow and Wolfie in hand. I put my pillow beside hers and she moves the cover and lays down, moving closer to the side of the bed to make room for me. I lay down beside her and she tucks me in with her cover. I feel safe here beside her in bed, like no one can harm me or touch me anymore, because my sister will kick their ass if they try. My eyes are heavy and I can't keep them open anymore. My body relaxes and I start to fall asleep.

- Sis, why did he do that? Did I do something wrong to him?

- Amalia... no you did nothing wrong, some adults just don't know what's right or wrong. Try to sleep now, and we will talk to mom in the morning when she wakes up and drinks her coffee.

I don't answer. Instead, I close my eyes and exhale, to make my body relax. My mind drifts back to everything that happened today with my mother's friend that just did all those things to me. I still don't know how to say this to mom because I don't understand it myself, these feelings I have now I have never felt before. It feels like something is crying inside me, and I can't make my mind stop spinning like a roller-coaster, just spiraling back through the whole night.

What did I do? Did I do something to make him do this? Or is this how it can be sometimes, just like my sister said? That some adults do stuff like this to children.

I lay still and trying to keep my eyes closed, but I can't help it, I keep opening them to stare at the door, to make sure that he doesn't come back and try this again. But now my sister is laying beside me, so she will protect me if something happens. The inside of my (little flower) hurts still and I could see blood on my panties, and I will ask mom about it tomorrow so it's nothing dangerous.

I drift off to sleep, and when I open my eyes again the sun is blazing through the window and the birds are singing and chirping outside.

I can hear someone slamming in the kitchen, and I realize that it's mom that is up, because she never sleeps in even when she can. I turn my head to the left to see if my sister also had gone up, but when I turn, I see that she has her back facing me and I can hear her breathing heavy, as she always do when she is sleeping.

I take off the cover and sit up on the side of the bed, putting both of my feet steady on the wooden floor, and turn my head to look towards the door, just to see so no one is there before I make my way to the bathroom. When I get close to the door I stop, just so I don't get too close before making sure once again that no one is outside of it. My legs start to shake, and I can feel a stone building inside my chest. I stand still so my body doesn't react more to me getting closer to the door. I try to understand why my body reacts like this, but I can't, the closest feeling similar to this, is when my sister made me watch Pet Cemetery 2 by Stephen King. I understand that I'm scared from yesterday, but I need to get to the bathroom before I pee myself.

I close my eyes and hold my breath to listen after footsteps or anything else that can give a hint if someone is out there. It really helps to close my eyes if I need to hear something important, because if I don't my mind goes somewhere else and I can't hear as good as I should. But I hear no sound of anything except my mom in the kitchen moving around and doing her morning routine, so I open the door to the hallway and look behind the door.

- Phew, empty

I step out, and make my way to the bathroom that is just wall to wall with my sister's room, so it's not far. I finally reach the toilet and I pull down my panties, and I can feel that they are sticky on the inside of them.

I glance down and take a deep breath to see why that is,

and I see more blood on them than I did yesterday, but it was dark then and now its bright outside, so I guess that makes a difference. And I was pretty shaken also by everything that I tried to wrap my head around, and I'm far from fine about all of this, but when we tell mom I will feel better.

I pull my panties up, wash my hands and make my way to my sister's room. She is still asleep, so I go to lay down beside her in bed, I want her to wake up soon so we can talk to mom. I exhale deeply and close my eyes, and as I close them I feel movement in the bed and my sister is turning to face me.

- Good morning, have you slept anything? she asks me.

- Yes a bit. Mom is awake now If you want to go down so we can talk to her? I say.

- I just woke up, so give me a minute to get my eyes back in my skull, I'm not even seeing clearly.

- Okey I'll wait. But I really want to go down, so I can go first if you like?

- No, Amalia, you' not going down before me because you can never shut up, and you will say it wrong and mom will be mad at us. So you wait for me and we go down together as I said last night.

- Fine,

I say and cross my arms pouting for a bit while she gets up and puts on clothes.

She puts on her clothes and then turns to look at me, and waves for me to get up and walk with her down to the first floor. I jump of the bed and stand up and rush after her as she moves out of the room, crossing the hallway to get to the stairs that leads down to the first floor. I stay close behind her, debating if this really is a good thing or not. Maybe this was just something that grown ups do to children, and that this just never happened to me before.

- You ready, Amalia?

she says without looking down on me as we leave the stairs and start to walk into the kitchen, where mom sits under the kitchen fan, smoking and drinking her morning coffee.

I just nod my head, afraid to speak because my stomach feels like it's turning inside out, as I get closer to mom. My sister is so cool for doing this, she really stands up for me this time. As sisters we fight sometimes, but I never feel like she doesn't love me.

She is four years older than me, so she doesn't like to play with me that much, but that never stops me from trying to nag her ears off until she gives in and plays with me for a bit.

When we enter the kitchen I take a look around, and I can see beer cans and wine bottles standing everywhere on the counters, the kitchen table is full of bowls of chips and plates with old food from yesterday. I think mom will have a full day cleaning this up today, she hates when the house is messy, or maybe she just loves to clean because she is always cleaning or rearranging furniture here at home.

- Good morning, mom, my sister says as we move closer to where mom is sitting.

- Good morning, my darlings. Did you two have a good night? We didn't wake you up with the music? mom asks us.

My sister looks down on me with a worry in her eyes, and I can see her eyes watering as she wraps one arm around me and takes a deep breath before she says anything. I just stay in her arm, close to her, and wait for what is coming next.

- Mom? she says with a low cracking voice.

- Yes, hun? What's wrong? Has something happened?

- We need to tell you something that happened to Amalia yesterday.

-Yes, of course. Did something happen here at home, or out when she was playing outside?

My sister goes silent for a minute, before she goes on telling mom what happened last night. As she begins I can feel my heart racing, and that reminds me of the feeling I had when I was going to the bathroom this morning, My head starts to spin back to everything that he said to me when he touch me that way, even when I said no.

- So I woke up in the middle of the night because I heard whispering, and Amalia trying to get someone away. And when I sat up in the bed to look if Amalia had a bad dream again, I saw a big shadow sitting beside her in the couch. I yelled at him to get

the hell out, and asked what he was doing here. He just stood up and laughed when he left the room.

When he was gone I rushed to Amalia, that started to cry, and she told me that he touched her in places no one can touch you, just like you always say mom.

Mom looks at me, but doesn't say anything. So I step forward, in front of my sister, to show mom the bloody panties, for her to understand better where he touched me.

- I said NO more than once, mom, and I really tried to get away from him, but he held my leg very hard so I couldn't move anywhere. I promise I really tried, mom. Please don't get angry with me. I didn't know what he was doing at first, and he was so kind and nice the whole night. At first I thought he wanted to play fun for a while, he said that everyone was leaving soon. But then he started doing these thing to me and I got scared. When his fingers entered me, the pain was to much and it was then I heard Wilma shouting out in the room for him to get out.

Mom's eyes widen and she looks at us with confusion, trying to speak, but her voice studders and cracks. She lights a new cigarette, puts it down on the ashtray, before standing up to go and pour a new cup of coffee. Me and Wilma stands in the same spot, waiting for a response to what we just told her. My pulse is hitting me hard and I can hear it beating. Wilma is tense, but she holds me close and I can feel her hand gripping my upper arm harder, before she asks mom if she heard what we said. Mom just stares out into space, takes a sip from the cup before she starts talking.

- Wilma, are you really sure that you saw things

right? It was late, and you were asleep and you know that Amalia has nightmares and is sleepwalking sometimes. Are you sure that it wasn't Amalia coming back to bed, and that she was dreaming?

- What? No, mom… I know what I saw, and he was sitting beside her doing bad things to her, I swear. The way Amalia cried was nothing like when she has her nightmares, I promise.

I can feel my head spinning, and the feeling of mom not believing us makes my heart feel strange, like a cold feeling goes from the heart out in my arm, and I can't stop myself from crying because it hurts inside my heart. I wipe my tears from my face with the back of my hand so I can see clearer. Wilma's face have dropped and she isn't facing mom anymore, she just stares at the floor. She looks defeated and I don't like when she looks like that. I breath in, trying to find courage enough to say something to her.

- Mom,

I say with sadness rushing over me, and I show her my panties again andrepeat myself on what he did to me. But she doesn't say anything, she just keeps smoking, staring into the kitchen fan. After a few minutes of silence from both Wilma and mom, my crying stops, making me feel uncomfortable and like a liar. Mom puts out her cigarette, puts down the cup and turns to face me before she takes my hands.

She grips them like she always does when she has

something bad to tell me, like when I've done something wrong.

- Amalia, darling, you are at that age when getting to know your body is interesting. So if you tried to put something in there to see what happens, I understand, but to try and blame someone else for it is not okay, Amalia. You understand that, right?

My face drops, facing the floor, trying to get my head around what she just said. Is she saying that I made this up? That I did this to myself? I can't understand why she is saying these things to me.

- Mom, no, I didn't do this to myself. I don't even know why things go up there. The pee comes from there.

- Oh, Amalia... there is more to that area, but you're too young for that kind of talk, and I don't want to give you new ideas for you to experiment on yourself. But this man is a good, good friend of ours, and he would never do something like that to anyone. He is one of the kindest people I know and I have known him for years. He was playing with you all evening, both of you having a laugh, so I find this really hard to believe.

I can feel how I go numb inside, and the sadness I felt minutes ago is gone. And I face my sister to see that she is faced by all of this. Mom continues to look at me like she wants me to say that I made it all up, but I can't say what she wants me to. I can hear the birds outside singing, so I focus on that instead of the cold air in here.

- Amalia, did you hear me?

Mom says, but I'm too far away in my head, just listening to the birds, for me to answer her right away.

She grips my hand and pulls me in to sit in her lap, but my body just wants to run away from that feeling. I don't want her to hold me at all, not after everything she said to me. I start to wiggle my body, trying to break free from her, but she is also too strong, and she wraps her arms around me trying to soothe me.

- Amalia, calm down and just listen to me, hun, she says with a low voice, but I can't stop myself trying to break free from this.

- Let me go!

I say out loud, while continuing to get away from her. My thoughts are running around in my head, trying to understand if what happened was just a dream or not. How do I explain the blood? The pain? Did I do this in my sleep? Why would mom not believe us?

- Amalia, calm down… shhh. Mom is not angry, so you can tell me if you experimented on yourself. Many children do, so that is nothing to be afraid of. Just tell mommy what you put up there, so I can take it away.

- I didn't do this to myself, mom, I've told you. Why don't you believe me? I say as I manage to break free from her holding me. I start to run up to my room, hearing mom calling me, saying like she always do when she thinks I've done something bad.

- Fine, Amalia, go to your room then. If you

don't want to tell the truth now, you'll be grounded for telling lies like this... Hope you understand that we are not finished talking about this.

I run up the stairs and into my room, throwing myself on the bed, feeling ashamed and dumb for all of this. I'm so stupid, and I hear his words mixed with my mom's inside my head, repeating everything; how wrong I am, and that I shouldn't lie like this.

My heart stills and the pain inside disappears, and a feeling of emptiness closes in on me, feeling scared everywhere in the house. I close my eyes as I try to sleep a bit; my mind drifts away to sleep, and the only noise I hear is the sound coming from the kitchen.

11

ROCK BOTTOM

B. A. MCCLUSKEY

Suicide

Abuse

Homophobia

Thirty years and a rope around my neck before I spoke my truth
Thirty years of hiding every fractured piece of youth
My father built our home from fear and sharpened every word
Until the sound of my own heart became something absurd
He told me if I loved men too, he'd put me in the grave
As if a son could choose the tides his lonely body gave
Those words sank deep like rusted nails driven through tender bone
And every year, I felt myself grow colder and alone
I learned to change the way I walked and how I moved my wrists
Learned how to laugh at hateful jokes and still pretend they missed
I dated women I adored, yet still felt split apart
Because another truth kept beating hidden in my heart

I looked at men with quiet eyes, then
punished myself after
Turned every spark of tenderness to
something filled with horror
Bisexual was not a word I dared to say
aloud
It felt like standing center stage while
shame addressed the crowd
Rock bottom came in fragments not a
single thundered fall
It lived inside the silence growing mold
along the walls
In every lie I told myself just to survive
the day
And every prayer begging these feelings to
decay
One night he saw too much in me and rage
consumed his face
The hallway light above us turned our
home into a cage
He wrapped his hands around my throat
and slammed me to the ground
And suddenly the whole damn world became
a muffled sound
His fingers crushed against my neck while
panic filled my chest
The ceiling blurred above my eyes as
darkness slowly spread

I clawed against his wrists and heard him
spit those words again
As if my life was something he could snuff
out there and then
I thought that I would die beneath that pale
and buzzing light
A frightened son still begging just to make
it through the night
And when he finally let me go I curled
against the floor
While he walked off like nearly killing me
was nothing more
After that I feared the sound of footsteps
near my door
I learned survival sometimes means
becoming less and less
I carried shame like chains wrapped tightly
underneath my skin
And every mirror held a man I did not
know within
Thirty years of burying every truth
beneath my tongue
Thirty years of feeling like I'd failed before
I'd begun
Thirty years of asking God why I was born
this way
As if the love inside my chest was
something to betray

Then one night came the rope and all the dark I could not fight
A lonely room a shaking chair a soul too tired to write
I tied the knot with trembling hands convinced that this was peace
Because I could not see a world where fear would ever cease
The ceiling fan above me spun like judgment in the gloom
And every hateful thing he said still echoed through the room
I thought about the child in me still desperate to be heard
Still choking on the silence wrapped around each unsaid word
Then something broke before my neck ever could that night
A tiny stubborn piece of me still reaching for the light
And standing there with rope in hand I finally understood
No one should have to die because they love more than one could
So I collapsed instead and cried until I could not stand
Years of grief came pouring out like water through my hands

And for the first time in my life I let the whole truth live
Not half a truth not watered down not something to forgive
I am bisexual and I will not disappear in shame
I will not carve myself apart to make you more okay
The room stayed standing when I spoke no fire filled the air
Only decades worth of chains grew lighter standing there
Then death came slow for him the way the winter swallows leaves
Quiet as the guilt some men refuse before they leave
And when I heard he finally died I sat there cold and still
Not mourning him but mourning all the things he chose to kill
I drove across the country with that lotion by my side
Miles of broken memories and sleepless nights to ride
Gas stations glowing through the dark like tired roadside stars
While thirty years of bruises rattled loudly in the car

Through desert heat and pouring rain I
carried every scar
Past empty fields and little towns and dim
forgotten bars
Because some journeys are not made for
closure or for peace
Some roads are built so haunted boys can
finally be released
And if he'd lived to see my children drawing
breath and light
I never would have let him near their hearts
or near their lives
No child of mine would ever learn to fear
themselves at home
Or feel their spirit shrinking every time
they stood alone
I'd never let his poison reach the softness in
their chest
Never let his hatred teach them they
deserved less
Because the cycle ends with me no matter
what it takes
And love should never leave a child
convinced their soul's mistake
At the funeral they praised him like a saint
returned to God
While I remembered every bruise and every
threat and sob

I stood beside his casket dressed in black from head to toe
And saw the man who made me fear the truth I now could show
Then from my pocket quietly I pulled the bottle free
Cheap lotion from the dollar store still cracked along the seam
I dropped it on his casket hard the sound cut through the room
Like every buried truth I had now finally in bloom
I smiled sharp as survival there beneath the churchyard glow
And said you'll be ashy where the hateful bastards go
Then turned my back and walked away into the open night
Still scarred but finally unafraid to stand inside my light

12

EVIL DOCTOR

SCARLETT INK

medical trauma

I had asked Dr Douchecanoe if I could get some ice to suck on whilst having treatment, and also when my cardiologist would be arriving.

Cause of my heart, my cardiologist was always there.

Dr Douchecanoe brushed me off, letting me know that ***I didn't need my cardiologist and that he'd get a nurse to bring ice because it wasn't his job.***

Yep.

He said those words.

Anyway, he continued with getting me set up with another nurse assisting – who also told him my cardiologist is supposed to be in attendance.

Dr Douchecanoe dismissed her.

He finally finished hooking me up and started my infusion.

Two minutes later my cardiologist walks in and asks Dr Douchecanoe why he hadn't been informed of my arrival?

The fucking Dr Douchecanoe LIED and said *'no one had told him that he needed to be here!'*

With steam billowing out my ears, I piped up, "I asked where you were and when you'd be here, and was dismissed!"

And also that the nurse had mentioned it.

Well, Dr Douchecanoe got very huffy and stuttered about patients being *'over dramatic.'*

Backpedalling furiously.

To which my cardiologist replied,

'Well I'd be a little *over dramatic* too if chemo had caused me two heart attacks in the past'.

My cardiologist asked Dr Douchecanoe to step outside with him, and I could hear the yelling from my room.

Turns out the nurse went and called him.

13
AMY

LLIANNE OLIVO

Graphic violence and murder

Drug use and addiction (including needles)

Toxic and abusive relationships (emotional and physical)

Sexual coercion, degradation, and power imbalance

Eating disorders and body image issues

helpline

988 suicide & crisis lifeline

call or text 988 or chat via 988lifeline.org

support for emotional distress, crisis, or suicidal thoughts (24/7, free, confidential)

samhsa national helpline

call 1-800-662-help (4357)

treatment referrals and support for substance use and mental health (24/7)

national domestic violence hotline

call 1-800-799-7233 or text start to 88788

help for anyone experiencing abuse or unsafe relationships (24/7, confidential)

rainn

call 1-800-656-hope (4673) or chat at rainn.org

support for sexual assault survivors (24/7)

crisis text line

text home to 741741 (u.s.)

free, confidential text support for any crisis (24/7)

AMY

LILIANA

All I can hear is Amy's tits slapping one another as she bounces up and down while Gabe pounds into her. She's doing the reverse cowgirl position. Facing me while I record them both for tonight's shoot. I'm supposed to upload this video by the end of the night. I keep having to start over and reset the angles because they don't stop fighting each other over the stupidest things. I, as the older adult in here, should have the right to tell them what to do if only they would listen.

It's late. It's hot, and sweat is running down my back. It doesn't get any cooler in July. Miami is never cool. I wasn't supposed to stay here another year, but if I don't help Oliver run the studio, he'd probably sell it and go back to selling drugs. I had to pull them up from that. I'm still addicted to it. If I don't get fucked or high or both, I'm a mess. I'm the worst person you want to be around when I'm mad, and these two are pissing me off.

I'm going to take a deep breath and focus on the lenses. "Slow down, Gabe. Keep one hand on her hip and the other on her tit. Play with her nipple.

When your hips are coming up, try to make it seem like you're squatting. Put energy into it."

He rolls his eyes and throws his head back. A fucking teenager. They are eighteen, but they behave as if they weren't taught any manners. Amy moans with her mouth open. Her cunt dripping. The lips of her vulva are swollen. Face red. She's about to squirt, and I need to capture that. That's what pays the rent. When there's fluid.

"Pluck her nipples, "I look at Gabe, then at both of them, "I want you both to cum at the same time. Then I want you, Gabe, to lift her up slowly so that she can drip and I can capture that on video. I don't want to have to do this scene again. I'm hungry, and I need my needles."

I feel the air leave my nose. Like a line shot through the night. It's just air, and I know I'm wet from making the video. Gabe's good-looking, and he's got that youthful skin. His penis is long and thick; you can count the veins. He works out whenever we are not making porn, and he spends most of his time in the studio. I like him. I just don't like eyerolls. I don't like his attitude.

Amy has to work as much as him to be able to make the money, and I have to work too. Our website is buried in the dark web, but our categories don't discriminate.

Amy's screaming. Gabe's groaning. I can see his handprints on her hips. I want to finger myself so bad. I know I'm going to hit my dildo or Gabe's dick or even Oliver's dick after I'm done with my needles tonight. I need one of them. It's hard to do this all day and not be horny. "Stop pulling my hair!" Amy shouts.

"Stop being such a tight cunt. You stupid bitch." Gabe responds like he's grinding his teeth.

I get closer to them. Right in front of the couch. Len's focused on her cunt. "Shut up. Moan. Lift her up and argue later. You two can tear each other apart later once I'm done. I'm fucking serious right now."

"I need a break. I want to wipe myself." Amy says. Panting and out of breath. Her chest is swollen at this point. Her lips are red, and she's covered in sweat. Gabe lifts her up, and I capture the moment her pussy excretes his cum like cream. He holds her until it's all come out.

"Good job. Amy, go clean and come to the bar later." Gabe puts her down, and she finds her legs. Wobbling. Making her way to the bathroom like she's got the widest thigh gap. He sits there, legs wide open, leaning against the backrest of the couch like he deserves it. "I'm so fucking tired of you calling Amy names. You know how that makes her feel. I hate how you make her feel. She already throws up right after she eats because she thinks she's too fat for you. Amy is perfect. She's small but curvy. She's the right amount of everything wherever it needs to be. You already made her bleach her hair. She had to cut it short because of that. You don't know how much your words affect her. She's your primary scene partner, and you should be treating her with respect."

He laughs like I told him a joke. "Respect? You make her eat you out every night. You make her lick your feet and eat your toes. And I'm the bad one for telling her she's a whale when I'm the one who has to lift her up for the frontals you want." He shot up, rubbing his dick soft. I put the camera down and walked in front of him.

"I write your check, you little shit. Just because you've got pretty eyes and penis that can last all day doesn't mean you get to say anything about what I do. You work for Oliver. You work for me. I get to tell you what to do, and I get to do whatever I want to you." I poke his abdomen. The motherfucker son of a bitch is ripped. Covered in tattoos but rock solid. "Now turn your fucking ass around and bend over."

I can tell he wants to challenge me, but he knows what's good for him. I'm regretted by his round ass. Two cheeks I grope and fondle and spank. "Meow for me."

He does. Soft and sweetly. "Wiggle your butt. Tell me who owns you."

"You own me. I'm your little cat. I'm always going to be your little cat."

I spit on his ass, then bury my finger. "I want you to cum when I say so. Then I want you to go find Amy and apologize to her. You're going to do whatever she wants, then you're going to come back to me and do whatever I want. Especially if you want me to keep sending your videos to that other studio you keep saying you'll leave us for."

He nods. Using the palm of his hands to balance himself out. I bury another finger, then finger fuck him until I hear him make noise. Not the wet sound but the moans. I like moans. They are better than street noise or sirens. When my mother died, there were too many sirens, and I just didn't want to be home. Everyone came over to find her dead on the floor on a puddle of her own blood. My dad had stabbed her with a butcher's knife, then ran out the door like a piece of shit. I was under the table in the fetal position.

That was my last day of school. My aunt moved, and everything was okay again, but then she started to bring men home. Too many of them. Some who wanted to sleep in my room, in my bed. Her door opened once every hour after 5 pm. Oliver lived across the street in the junk yard with his dad, selling body parts. Car body parts. At this point, we may as well be dealing with the black market with the types of pornography these people are asking me for. Oliver took me from my aunt's. I turned 14. He was the only one who didn't touch me or take anything from me, but he gave me drugs. I sold them, and I used them. I used too much.

The only way I can calm down is if there is something inside of me or if I get to do whatever I want to Gabe and Amy. When they look hopeless and miserable, I'm happy.

I've stretched out Gabe's ass so bad I can fit three fingers. His moans became cries and whimpers. His breathing head and settled deep in his throat. "Cum, little cat."

"Oh my god, Lili. My dick's about to blow up." He shoots a load into the couch and finishes rubbing it off. Then he kneels and licks it off the cushion. I'm not expecting to find any drops. I rub the top of his head and wipe my fingers on his hair.

"Good boy. I'm heading to my room to edit and upload. When you're done with Amy, tell her to come to me. If you see Oliver, tell him to come to me." Gave nods, getting off the floor, walking away from me, and rubbing his behind.

I take the camera and then walk up to my room. I open my door and take off my robe. It's black silk. A couple of red roses were painted on it. I walk in front of the mirror. My nipples are hard. My pussy lips are dripping wet. I'd have fucked Gabe, but I just didn't want him tonight. Sometimes he's just disgusting to me.

I work better under the red light. Even if I'm not processing the photos I took of the couch before we began. I plugged the camera into the computer. I watched the videos for today. Multiple takes. Some clips are longer than others. I edit the lighting, the shadows, and the skin imperfections that I can see. Freeing my curls from the updo. I use both hairclips to pin my nipples. I let them hang from them. Feels good to pretend not to feel it. I find my clit with the hand I don't need and I watch Amy. Her pussy. Her tits. Her mouth. She's perfect in every way that hurts. I can't wait for her to come to my room. I want to kiss her. I want to caress her hair. I want us to watch the video be upload. She's the queen of tags on that fucking pornsite. I want her to kneel. I want to put chains around her body. I want her to look confused and hungry at the same time. My hands are tingling just for the thought. My clit is so sensitive and moist. Fingers are coated in me. I open the drawer under the desk with the drugs. Another needle for my jugular. It'll make the sirens stop.

I haven't eaten anything today. I had a little coffee. I weigh less than I did last month. It's the drug. I wanted to lose weight and relax, but now I feel like I might break if the wind finds me. My face is pale, and my brown eyes look gone in the mirror. I gotta talk to Oliver about it whenever he comes home.

Where's Oliver?"

GABE

"Open the door, you fucking cunt!" I bang my hands on the frame. Feeling Lili's fingers still in my ass. I swear she forgets what she does when her mind takes over. I don't really know her that much. But she brings out the little in me. Amy brings out the beast. She opens the door, finishing a line of cocaine on her wrist. "I got fingered while you're in here turning white. Don't finish my fucking powder, you bitch."

I grab her by the neck and slam her against the wall. "Gabe, stop! I was on that couch for hours. I need to get high so I don't get hungry so I don't get fat because you're always calling me fat."

"Yeah, you are fucking fat. You don't even know how to put on clothes after a shoot. Shower and put on shorts at least. You never know when you're going to give Oliver or Lili a suck."

She jerks off, but I don't let her go. I'm holding her with both hands now. I'm lifting her above the ground, and I'm squeezing hard. She went from looking high to looking horrified. "Who's your daddy?"

"You're my daddy. I'm daddy's little girl. I'm always going to be daddy's little girl." She responds in that sweet voice. I like that sweet, low little voice.

I choke her tighter. Until her eyes water. Nipples hard. That's how I know she likes it. She loves it when I choke her. That's why I make the sex scenes last longer. I can get more time with her. Otherwise, Lili is all over Amy. She doesn't like to share her pets. "Kiss me with that powdery breath."

She does. Our lips clashed. Our tongues curl. My cock is already hard. From fucking. From finger fucking. From touching Amy. "Ride my knee," I offer it to her. She sits on it. Her cunt makes my skin feel so sticky. She begins to move. I begin to squeeze and squeeze. Sucking face and biting lips. "If you want to cum, you're going to promise me you're not going to eat anything until I say so." I looked into her eyes. "You're going to tell Oliver you can't play with him tonight. You're going to tell Lili your head hurts and you want to stay in your room because you took too much powder. Because you're sore. Because of me. Blame it on me."

I can't tell if she's nodding or having a seizure. Her eyes are full of tears. I slam my knee against her cunt. "Say yes, Daddy."

She trembles. Her thighs are shaking. I get a little, "Yes, Daddy."

"Kneel and keep my balls warm." I let go of her knee, and I remove my knee from under her. She's on her knees before I could blink. Kneading my nutsack. Swallowing half of it. Then the rest. Till her mouth is stuffed. I look around her room. She used to be a cheerleader in high school before she joined us. A flyer. Her boyfriend broke up with her on her birthday, and she came here to do mouth auditions with me. I think I have some sort of attachment to her. Even though I'm trying to fight whatever this is.

Amy made these four walls her home. Bookshelves. Cheerleading portraits. Pictures of some dogs I've never seen her bring here. She doesn't hang up her porn video thumbnails like I do. She hangs up dried flowers from Lili's garden. The coolest thing is her cocaine plate. I can tell she's been hitting it for a while.

I look down at her and find her staring back at me. Maybe at the tattoos. Maybe at the boy I used to be before we started to do whatever we wanted with each other. Those are the rules of the house. Everybody fucks everybody. The only time we don't is when the girls are on the moon. But even then, Oliver and I bone. I like it when we make porn like that. When it happens naturally, and everyone is naked on the floor.

"No, don't use tongue. I don't want to hear your voice. Just saliva. I just want my balls warm. Nod if you understand," I lift a brow. She nods. And I smile because watching her mouthful of cock gives me so much joy. Her eyes are poking out from how stuffed she is. My hips move instinctively. Towards her. The back of her head hits the wall. I thrust again. She gaps and chokes. Gagging on me. I take that as an invitation to continue. I close my eyes and fuck her mouth like I don't care if I kill her.

I like the sounds she makes. Like she's living in a horror movie and not in a porn house. My balls are telling me I'm close. My hips are telling me I'm tired. I've been fucking since I woke up. Lili's always trying to find the right angles, and nothing makes the cut. She just makes us do it again. On the couch, on the counter, on the bed. I didn't come here because I wanted to get high. I came because of Oliver. He used to be my favorite pornstar. I'd jerk off to his videos every night when I was in school. Oliver Star, featuring Liliana Ramos. Oliver's so hot. I wish Amy's mouth were his ass. I wanted to become a pornstar so that one day I could be his. But deal with darker things than just porn. We satisfy darker needs.

I wish he were here right now. I wish I had him behind me. Pounding me. Amy bites me before my imagination makes me cum. "You fucking bitch. You ruined my orgasm. I never ruin yours. You bitch!" I grab her face and smack the back of her head against the wall. She screams. Pushing me off her. I don't fall at first, but the next push does it. "I'm going to kill you! Fat bitch!"

"Leave me alone, please!" She bolts for the door. Opening it with squirrel hands. I'm coming right behind her at the same speed. I chase her across the hall to Lili's door. Lili opens the door. Amy stumbles and crawls into the room like a rat. Before I see the metal bat, Lili hits me with it, and my vision goes black. All I feel is the next smack and the next smack. Then nothing.

AMY

My throat hurts and burns. I wanted to projectile vomit on him. I can't believe he'd use me like that. Make me feel like I was just a hole for his cock. That this hole had no feelings or a mind of its own. I couldn't breathe. I didn't want to bite him. I liked Gabe a little. I don't think he liked me. It doesn't matter now because he's bleeding out on the floor and Lili is on top of him. Smashing a bat onto his skull. She's senseless. She sounds like an animal. He sounds like blood, flesh, and bone. Lifeless.

I don't think she's going to stop. I'm not even going to ask her to. I'm going to wipe my mouth and hide behind the door until Oliver gets home. He always fixes everything. He kept Gabe under control. Gabe and I only had one job: Fuck on camera when Lili wanted. All we had to do was fuck. But he stripped so much away from me, I don't even know who I am.

It's not easy to watch the boy you just fucked die. My first gig was giving him a blowjob. My second gig was giving Oliver a blowjob. My third gig was eating Lili out. That's how I got hired. That's how I got my home. This studio. I didn't want to go to college after my best friend posted my nudes on the class's Facebook group. He said he loved me. He wanted to prove it. Said that having sex in front of a camera was the way to go. The next day comes, and everyone is texting me my nudes. He broke up with me and called me a whining bitch. My parents found out.

When I graduated, I told them I didn't want to go to college. I wanted to stop being afraid of the camera. My mom knows what I do for a living and where I live. I grew up with two golden retrievers. My mom didn't want me to keep at least one. I learned to stop being attached to anyone and anything. But I failed because I'm attached to Gabe and I miss him.

I wanted to be perfect for him. He would do all kinds of things to me. Make me lick the toilet seat after he used it. Make me starve myself for days so I wouldn't weigh anything. He made me sleep with his cock in my mouth so it wouldn't get cold. I liked sleeping with him. I just didn't like him treating me like trash. I kind of like the fact he's no longer hurting, but I feel bad for liking it.

Lili has stopped. She's straddling his motionless body. She's got blood splashed all over her face, her hair, and her breasts. The bat is covered in blood and probably bits and pieces of Gabe's brain.

I come crawling over to her side. Licking my lips, wetting my tongue. "Lili? Are you okay? What are we gonna do now?" I tap her shoulder. She's in limbo.

"I'm sorry you had to see that, Amy. I hated this motherfucker. I told him to do whatever he wanted to you, but I didn't tell him to make you scream," she wasn't looking at me. She was looking at him. She looked angry and pissed. "Only I say when you get to scream. You're mine."

I exhaled and offered my hands to try and help her off him, "no, Amy. I'm going to sit on his soft dock. Then I'm going to smash it with the bat and rip it apart." Again, she wasn't looking at me. I just swallowed my breath and tried not to freak out.

"Do you want to cuddle up on the couch while we decide what to do, Lili? Do you want me to help you clean up?" I asked, just trying to keep it together, and because at the end of the day, I love Lili. She knows exactly what kind of treatment I need, and she knows how to get the little girl out of me. Sometimes I need that kind of harm. That kind of pain and humiliation. I just didn't lie when Gabe did it. He was cruel.

It takes me a minute, but Lili gets up and off him, wiping the blood off her tits with one hand and grabbing my wrist with the other. She looked into my eyes. Then she kissed me. I kissed her back. She breaks the kiss and starts to cry. I shake my head. "I'm okay, Lili. He's dead. He won't be hurting me anymore."

"I know. You don't hate me, right? This life is shitty. The studio is shitty. I haven't even cooked you a meal." She cried, telling me about her insecurities. About the storm currently wrecking her inside.

I kiss her again, then I rub my nose against hers, "I love you, Lili. You don't cook, but you buy me drugs, and that's what I like. Plus, we get the best of the best. I love you and Oliver. You're my family. We'll find another boy. In the meantime, we'll make the content and keep the website afloat." I nod to her with a smile on my face.

"You're more put together than I am. I thought you'd leave after this, Amy. You might be young, but you're strong. Maybe even stronger than me," I tap her lips with a finger.

"No. You're stronger. You brought him down with a couple of blows. You killed him for me. He was fucking the life out of my throat, and I almost passed out. Gabe never liked me for me—"

The door to the porch opened, and Oliver walked in. He blinked when he saw Gabe's body on the floor. "Are you serious, Lili? You do this again?"

Lili lets go of my wrist right away. She walks up to Oliver and leans into his embrace, "I'm sorry. He was hurting Amy. Gabe's been pissing me off for a while now. I know you really liked that boy." Oliver's neck was the place she buried her face.

"Honey, I didn't like Gabe. I just made him believe whatever I wanted him to believe so I could get ass on cam. That boy was a toy. Amy's family.

Aren't our girl, Amy?" he asked, looking into my eyes.

I smile and feel my cheeks burn. Not from the blowjob, but to find out that I actually mattered to them. "I'm your girl. Every part of my body is yours, but what are we going to do with the body?"

Lili's head comes up, "feed him to the zombies, cut him up in pieces, and sprinkle glitter on him. Toss him into a meat grinder." My eyes open so wide they hurt.

"Well, you say that so easily..." I feel like I'm swallowing a rock whenever I want to clean my throat. I begin to pace, and the back of my neck starts to itch.

"She's killed before. I'll just use HF on a tank. I keep lots of it in the basement just in case we need to get rid of a dealer. Lili killed the couple who used to make movies with us. They set up a pornsite behind our backs. Lili found out and cut their throats when they got high. I cleaned it up," he said, as if it were something you do every day. I get a little scared, but at the same time, nothing is making me want to run away.

Oliver let go of Lili because she was trying to move again. She comes back to me and takes my hand, this time without just grabbing the wrist, "I told you. You'll hate me. I have a hard time not getting rid of people if they piss me off. Those two betrayed us after we gave them a roof, drugs, and sex. But I promise I won't do it in front of you, next time." She kisses my forehead.

I grope her breast and twist her nipple. I lick Gabe's blood off my fingers. "You wanna use the double dildo while Oliver cleans?"

"That's not what you call it, but yes!" Her face brightens up. I shake my head and laugh. I'm never going to get it right. Lili caresses the top of my head. "Bring my needle. I need it."

I nod and go to Lili's, searching for the dildo. She's got a toy trunk of animal-shaped phalluses. Dildos shapes and sizes I still cannot understand. I pick up the purple one because it's long, thick, and veiny. Reminds me of Gabe's dick. I find Lili's heroine case and make my way out of the room. She's already preparing to take the shot. Oliver brings gallons upon gallons labeled 'hydrofluoric acid', placing them around Gabe's body. He isn't paying much attention to us, but I know he's looking in case we need anything. Lili hands me a bottle of lube, and I hand her the case.She works on her shot while I rub lube all over the dildo. Thoroughly.

My favorite thing is to suck on these. Before we use them. That's how I learned how to suck. Damn it. I forgot the nipple clasps that give me electric shots when I press the button on the tiny remote. But Lili took her shot, and she's coming towards me. She pins me against the counter of the bar. Her kisses are passionate, breathless, and hard. We grope each other's breasts and wrestle with tongues. And suddenly my night has just gotten better. I can taste Gabe's blood in my mouth and her saliva. "Are we rolling?"

She shakes her head and barely says, "not while we are trying to dissolve the body. But tomorrow, once the living room is cleaned up."

OLIVER

I've been married to Lili for twenty years. Her killings began in middle school when she drowned the little girl who told her I was her boyfriend. Lili didn't want to share me. Not even when we got old enough to have sex. It took me years to talk her into sharing, into making film, and seeing how incredible our lives were going to be. Amy has been a great addition. She's ours. She taught Lili how to share. I honestly thought that girl wouldn't last in a place like this. Let alone survive Lili. Somehow, we allowed Gabe to be here for as long as he was, to try to think that he was more powerful than me. That piece of ass.

I shake my head as I remember him. When we first fucked. He looked like he had fallen in love. I can't blame the boy. I'm hot. My life is hot. I get to watch the girls make out and get ready to have some fun. I'm going to be dissolving Gabe's body here. I need my gloves. I need my mask. I gotta change to long sleeves. But watching Lili and Amy get on all fours, buttcheeks against buttcheeks, that makes me want to stop what I'm doing so I can join in. The pool of blood is just chef's kiss. Fucking hate this boy for making Amy bleach her red hair blonde. That bastard makes my mouth taste bad.

I set the gallon of HF down and come up to the counter where Amy left the dildo so I can bring it to them. "You two look so pretty tonight. I'm gonna come up when I'm done with Gabe. Stay wet for me."

Lili smiles. She's high. Her brown eyes twinkle. "Shh. I'm playing with my favorite girl in the world. We'll handle you later." She winks.

Amy's giggling, playing with blood on the floor. I attach one end of the dildo to her pussy and the other end to Lili's pussy. I smack their asses. They buck against each other, and the sounds are perfect. This would make one hell of a video.

I watch them for a while. Licking my lips. Running a hand through my dirty blonde hair. The scene transforms the studio not a house of pleasure. They grind. Tits smacking. Mouths open like if they buck any harder, they're gonna scream. I get up slowly. I pick Gabe's body up by the arms and drag him out. I'm taking him downstairs, and then I'll come up for the gallons of HF.

14

FIRST EPISODE

SYLAS SEABROOK

Contains detailed thoughts about suicide and a positive overall message.

"Mom..." Tears rolled down my flush face as I cradled a knife in one hand. "I called to say goodbye. I can't handle it anymore. My life is over. I'm going to end it."

"Son, will"—er voice cracked—"will you do me one favor?"

"If it's not to not do it, yes. I'll give you that."

"No, it's not. I want you to go to the hospital."

It was a ridiculous request. What could the hospital do? I breathed in deeply enough to fill my chest, then sighed, my crying causing a full-body hiccup.

"Yes. I'll go."

"I love you, son. I love you."

"I love you too, Mom."

I climbed off my floor bed, leaving the knife behind; stood; and wiped the tears from my face. Breathe in, breathe out. I did. Again. Then I went to my housemate and asked him to take me to the hospital.

The trip gave me time to think, and I got lost in the whirlwind of thoughts…They were all depressing. The tree I had selected to die under became more enticing. I cried silently, earning stares from my housemate. I didn't answer his unasked question and let him drop me off at the hospital. He asked me when he should come back, and I gave him a weak shrug, hands up, then looked at him for what I thought would be the last time.

The guard at the door disavowed me of my lighter. Just another thing lost in this world. A finger pointed at a terminal guided me to check-in. It wanted to know why I was there. I wrote suicidal. They would probably just laugh me out of the hospital. At least I will have given my mom her last wish.

They came out rather quickly and ushered me down a hallway, deep into the hospital into what appeared to be a basement. I was urged to change into a gown—no drawn curtains—and given a bed to lay on in a row of such beds. These little divided areas had no electronics, no wires, no nothing but a bed and a chair. The duty nurse was able to see into every bed from his vantage point in the middle. It felt dehumanizing, but I understood why the precautions given how much my brain was focusing on dying.

I couldn't care less about my situation. It was just delaying the inevitable, so I slept.

And I slept.

Some time later—it was impossible to tell hours from days—the nurse approached.

"Your transportation is ready."

"Where am I going?"

"A mental health facility. We're going to help you get better."

"It won't work," I said with deep hopelessness.

If the nurse replied, I don't recall. I didn't care. Nothing they could say or do would change anything.

Some of us assigned a bed were put onto a bus that had backed up to the hospital and transported across town into a gate unloading area. Why did it have to be gated? Was where I was going that scary? If it was, they were in for a shock: I didn't care if I lived or died, so there was nothing they could do to me.

Check-in was boring, draining…all I wanted to do was sleep. A strip search (no cavity search, thank the Fates) and a change of clothes later and I was taken through a corridor into a main room with side rooms attached. Down the way on the left was my room. A two-person hospital room with just a solid wooden bed; a sheet, blanket, and pillow; and a thin mattress. When you're planning on dying, I guess you don't need anything.

I made the bed and laid down.

I slept.

And slept.

When I woke, it was breakfast time of some day —who knew which—so I followed the group of people into the mess hall. The food reminded me of high school slop, but it was edible, so I made do. I'm still not sure what all the food was.

We returned to the main area and everyone split off into groups. I didn't try to socialize; I sat at a round table by myself and cried. My thoughts raced further into the abyss of death. Where was hope? I had nothing to hope for.

I approached a counselor. "Can you talk?" I said, my voice hoarse.

He followed me back to the table, and I rambled on for some time, telling him about everything I had lost, how my life was over. That got me to thinking. I had helped so many over the years. If I could turn to any one person for help, it would be me, but that's like saying "healer, heal thyself."

"I'm the helper," I said. "Who helps the helper?"

The man listened, but didn't say much, just assuring me they would get me help.

Time went on. My sadness still reigned supreme.

"Sylas, you have a phone call. It's your daughter."

I blanched. How could I talk to her? What would I say? Either way, I couldn't not answer her call. I calmly walked over to the phone and with as much trepidation as I had just exhibited confidence, I answered.

"Daddy, what's wrong?" my sixteen-year-old asked me.

"My brain isn't working right. I don't know what's wrong, but I can't stop it. I'm getting help. Just give me some time, okay?"

It was a lie, but I couldn't tell her the truth: I was just waiting to get out to end my life.

"I'm here for you, Daddy. Always remember I love you."

There was more to the conversation, but my anguished heart didn't process it. My baby wanted to help, but Daddy was beyond help. It hurt more than a cut across the neck.

My boss came to visit. My friends came to visit. The conversations were dull and more about their curiosity at my situation than anything, but the did all offer to help—if they could. I was beyond help. How could anyone help me? I couldn't even help me.

I made some "friends" in the mental hospital. Guys who had it just as hard as me. My roommate had been disowned by his family, had something mentally wrong such that he couldn't work, and had no friends...he'd isolated himself from everyone.

Another man had lost his wife, his life savings, and his job. Coupled with his excruciating pain and he was aching from flesh to spirit. I felt for him.

I felt for all of them, and true to form, I tried to help them all, mostly by listening and showing care. Someone to hear them and give a shit was all they really wanted. Who could do that for me?

I received calls from people all over. I sighed for each call. Why were they bothering me? Why were they trying to revel in my pain? Couldn't people just let me go in peace?

I sat in a chair, staring out the window and pondered. Who helps the helper? I closed my eyes with sublime realization and exhaled. There's a story about someone asking God to save them and ignoring all non-miraculous means of saving. When they die and go to heaven, they ask God why he didn't save them and he cites all the different ways of saving them that had come to them. Sometimes, the point is, we miss the help we are given.

My boss. My friends. My college buddies... Everyone I had helped was coming out to me. I finally had the answer to who helps the helper: all those he's helped.

A tear slipped from one eye, then the other, followed by a stream. Maybe with help, I could get through this. Maybe with help, I could get better. I just needed to let people help me and stop believing I was beyond help—as a helper, I'd never let anyone start with that premise, so why me?

TWENTY YEARS HAS PASSED since that time, and I was diagnosed Bipolar I. I'm now on a proper medicine regime and have learned how to better self-identify when bad situations arise. Life brings us challenges, and with the support of so many, we can get through them.

15

RESTRICTED

C. J. JENKINS

eating disorders

It was 1:57 a.m.

She glanced at the clock after finishing edits on one of her short stories. The familiar sound followed. A low rumble in her stomach.

Did I even eat dinner today?

The fact that she had to think about it was telling.

"Oh," she realized. "Cheese and crackers."

That didn't qualify as dinner, but hell, it was protein.

She told her editor she was tired. And hungry.

"Go eat something," he suggested.

She made a face.

He noticed but didn't press. By now, he knew better. Not because she was rude, but because her honesty could cut in ways people weren't always ready for. Not disrespectful. Just... direct.

She caught the look before he said anything. And if she was being honest with herself, something was starting again.

She didn't technically have an eating disorder. Not the kind people recognize immediately. But for lack of a better word, it was still disordered. She wasn't eating.

Restriction.

That was the word.

And it was a problem.

She weighed herself every day. That part wasn't new. But lately, it wasn't once a day. It was two, three, four times. First thing in the morning. After meals. Late at night. Everyone knows weight fluctuates, but that logic doesn't matter anymore.

The scale had become her addiction.

Which made sense. She had an addictive personality.

But worse than the scale was the pit in her stomach. The question she asked herself every night.

Do I ignore this and go to bed like I usually do? Drink some water, maybe tea, and keep the number low in the morning?

Or do I give in?

She knew it wasn't real weight gain. Just fluctuation. But knowledge didn't stop behaviour.

Food used to be something she enjoyed. Now it was transactional. Strategic.

She had it calculated.

If Kevin was coming to visit, she'd eat normally, healthy. Enough. He knew her too well. She couldn't slip around him.

Three days, she'd think. That's three days of meals.

When he left, she'd pull back again. One meal a day. Snacks if necessary. Ride the Peloton daily. Burn off whatever damage she thought she'd done.

She told herself she had control.

A week passed.

She stepped on the scale and froze.

143.

Her eyes narrowed. Not even a week ago she'd been at 150 even. Seven pounds didn't just disappear. Not without trying. Not without illness.

She stepped off. Reset it. Changed the batteries because obviously something had to be wrong.

She stepped back on.

142.8.

That was worse.

She walked to the mirror and really looked this time.

She could see her ribs.

Not in a good way more of

are you eating kind of way

Her face looked a little haunted. Not alarming. Nothing makeup couldn't hide. But she remembered the looks at the office. The careful ones.

Hey, how are you?

Concern layered with questions no one felt entitled to ask. Cancer. Sickness. Something serious.

She looked sick.

That's when she knew she couldn't do this alone.

She wasn't purging. That wasn't her pattern. But the restriction was enough. Seven pounds without trying. No illness. No explanation.

Her healthy weight hovered around 160. At 5'7", 142 didn't look thin.

It looked wrong.

She made an appointment with her therapist that day.

They talked honestly. He admitted it wasn't his specialty and referred her to a colleague. Over the next three months, they worked on repair. Nothing extreme. No punishment. Just enough food. Enough consistency. Enough care.

Only then did she connect the symptoms she'd been ignoring. The burning sensation. Food that tasted spicy when it wasn't. The quiet discomfort she kept brushing off as stress.

It was all related.

Repair didn't come easily, but it came deliberately.

Ninety days later, she stepped on the scale again.

153.

This time, she didn't rush away. She looked at her body instead. Her face had softened. There was color again. A glow she hadn't noticed was gone until it returned.

Standing there, she made herself a promise.

She would take better care of herself.

Because she was more than a number on a scale.

16

2664 DAYS

TWELVE HOURS THIRTY-SIX MINUTES, FROM DIAGNOSIS TO DEATH.

ALANA DAIL

grief

Twelve hours thirty-six minutes, from diagnosis to death.

That is how long it took for my life to change completely. Some days it doesn't feel heavy, but something will happen that makes me laugh.

Grief is funny that way.

I was cleaning out my jewellery box the other day and found the watch that my mother and I used to terrorize each other with.

Now, let me explain. I had the simplest watch; it had a light pink band, and I wore it at work. It's something that I grabbed at Walmart one day. Well, somehow I set an alarm on it, and to this day I still don't know how I did it. But it would go off every day at 1:17 pm. It was a high-pitched, repetitive beep. And it would go off for twenty-five minutes, unless you turned it off. When I finally moved out of her house, I left it in the bathroom cabinet. It took her several weeks to figure out what it was.

Then she brought it to me, but failed to tell me about the alarm. She didn't just bring it to me; she hid it in my apartment. I found it about two weeks later, called her, and we laughed for a long time. I made a smart ass comment about how I was going to bring it back and hide it. I did. From then on, it became a game; you never knew when you would get the watch back, but it always found its way back from one house to the other. Yes, this went on for years; the battery had been changed, and we kept it going. I always laugh when I think about that. That is how I choose to remember my mother. Not the time she got sick.

She started feeling sick around Halloween 2018. She kept complaining of a stomachache. At first, no one thought anything of it. We all thought it was something she ate at a restaurant, or that something wasn't settling right with her. As time went on, she continued to complain that it was getting worse. We started asking her to go to the doctor and figure out what was happening. She said it would get better on its own. I personally think she was afraid that they would tell her something was wrong.

Fast forward to Thanksgiving 2018. She was excited about it. I had taken over the cooking a few years before that, so she was always excited to come eat, help with the mess, then leave. She loved to cook, but Thanksgiving stressed her out. I took it over since I had the bigger kitchen, and she was grateful. As dinner approached, my father called, saying that my mom wasn't feeling well and wasn't hungry. I put my foot down that night with my dad. I said if she is too sick to come to dinner, she has to go to the doctor, and if he didn't take her, I was going to come and take her to the ER. Enough was enough, he agreed with me. Now, when it came to my mom, my dad was a pushover. It took another week to convince her to go to the ER.

December 1st, she walked into the hospital ER. They took her vitals, her backstory, and ran a number of tests. I didn't know it was worse than she was letting on. She had hardly eaten anything in over a month. I like to think she was sparing us the knowledge of how bad it was, like any mother would; she didn't want her kids to worry. The doctors said she needed to be admitted for more testing and scans. We were getting pieces of the puzzle, but no definitive course of treatment or diagnosis. I called and talked to her every day, and made the hour-long drive to the hospital multiple times.

Thinking that she was finally getting better. I finally was able to corner one of her nurses. I asked her about my mother's eating. She said she is not taking in much, so whatever she requested, we could bring her in. I asked if it got to bad if they were going to put in a feeding tube. The nurse looked shocked that I even asked that question, apparently she was not sick enough for that. Yet. I was in charge of keeping the rest of the family informed about what was going on. Most of my mother's family lives in California, so someone had to keep them up to date, and that fell on me. And I was fine with it.

December 13th, around 11:45 am, my father called and said that the doctors finally had a diagnosis. My mother had stage four lymphoma. Stage four. This had been going on for longer than anyone knew.

But that is the thing about cancer, it's there, and you might not ever know it. I asked to speak with my mother, he said that she was talking with the nurses, getting moved to the cancer wing of the hospital, that they didn't want to discharge yet, without having started treatment and having a plan in place. I of course had to call my cousins and let them know what was going on. They were hard phone calls to make. At this point, I was exhausted, my father was exhausted, but we had a diagnosis, and we finally had answers.

She was moved to the cancer wing, and she met her nurses, who were fantastic. I spoke with them and her oncologist on the phone. He didn't sugarcoat it; he said it was going to be a long, hard road ahead of her, but they were confident that they could start treatment within the next day or two. I spoke with her a few hours later, telling her that we had this, we had fought for things before in our family, this was just one more hurdle that we needed to face head-on. We were all in her corner, and she would not have to fight alone. I told her I loved her and that I would see her in the morning.

My father called me at almost midnight, saying that my mom was being moved to the ICU because she had started having trouble breathing. I was asleep, but jumped up quickly, throwing on whatever clothes I had lying on the floor next to my bed. I kissed my husband and told me I would call him when I knew something more. That hour drive seemed to only take me fifteen minutes. Let's face it, I was speeding, I knew in my gut that something was not right and I had to be there. When I got to the hospital, I met my father in the waiting room. He said they had just brought her up. Her oncologist nurse brought my mom's bag out to us and told us that my mother was being placed on a breathing machine.

To say that we were shocked is an understatement. She told us she was going to go in and check to see if we were able to go see her. A few minutes later, she came out and brought us to her room. I walked into her hospital room at 12:21 am. I saw my mother hooked up to all kinds of tubes and wires, including the one breathing for her. Her eyes were wide open. It was not like you see in the movies and TV shows, where they look like they are sleeping with a small tube in their mouth. It was horrifying to me. I couldn't keep looking at her.

I was in the corner of the room crying. Her

nurse came over to me, clearly seeing the panic attack coming on. She walked over to me, put an arm around my shoulders asking if I wanted to step out for a moment. I couldn't say anything, I only nodded. She walked me into the hallway, where I had a complete meltdown. I told her that was my mother's body, but she wasn't in there anymore. She looked at me, confused, saying that she was in there. I didn't believe her. My mother had always been so full of life, and that was not the person I saw lying in that bed. She asked if I wanted to go back into the room.

I shook my head, and she said I will sit with you in the waiting room for a bit. She walked me out there, held my hand while I cried, told stories through tears, snot, and shaky breaths. The next thing I remember was hearing a code blue for her room. Another nurse escorted my father out to the waiting room with me. The doctor came back and said that they had got her back. Thus began the longest five hours of my entire life. She coded several more times. Each time it was taking longer and longer to bring her back. Her oncologist came and talked with us, letting us know this. It was time for my father to make a decision. They could keep going, but with how long it was taking to bring her back each time, they were starting to get concerned about her brain function.

My father decided that the next time she coded

would be the last time. He didn't want her to suffer anymore. I was able to say my goodbyes to her, although I couldn't look at her. I believe when I saw her right after midnight, she was already gone. It's something that I believe to this day, her body was here, but she was not. I told her I loved her, that I would always talk to my kids about her, especially my youngest, who was just over a year old at the time.

I kissed and squeezed her hand and walked out of the room. My father stayed with her until she was gone. He came into the waiting room when she was gone; he was falling to pieces in front of my eyes, but trying to remain strong. The doctor came out and sat with us. Offering his condolences, he said something catastrophic had to have happened for her to go downhill so quickly.

People go to the hospital to get better, not worse. He talked more to my dad, and I was not hearing much of anything. I felt like I was underwater. I had to make phone calls to family in California, waking them up at nearly four am for them, telling them that their aunt was gone.

I had to track down her brother and tell him. I don't remember making phone calls, but I remember sitting on the floor near the elevators with my phone in my hand, crying. After the doctor left, we signed a bunch of papers, and it was done. My father asked me if I wanted to come back to the house. I told him no, I needed to get home to my husband and my kids, let them know what happened.

I don't remember the hour-long drive home. I can't tell you if I took the highway or the back roads. I just remember unlocking the front door, my husband walked into the kitchen, and I collapsed in his arms, crying. He asked what happened, all I could do was shake my head, and say gone. My kids had woken up by this time, and were confused and concerned seeing me like that. My husband picked me up and walked me outside until I calmed down.

He explained it as best he could to our kids, who were five and one at the time. I don't remember anything else that happened that day. I think I slept, I might have eaten, I might have gotten drunk. I honestly don't know. The world didn't stop. I kind of thought it should. I still have her number in my phone; I can't bring myself to delete it. I don't know if I ever will. I used to do this thing where every time I got in my car, I would call her. Even if I was taking a five-minute drive to the grocery store. I just wanted to talk to her. In the months that followed her death, I caught myself reaching for my phone whenever I got in my car.

I didn't know what do. It was surreal. I would laugh at the thought that I would never make one of those pointless, "Hey, Mom, I have chicken strips for lunch" phone calls again. Everyone says that there are five stages of grief, and we all know what they are. Denial, Anger, Bargaining, Depression, Acceptance. I honestly think that is BULLSHIT.

It's not some checklist you work through. Have I had all of those feelings? Yes, but sometimes they come back up out of nowhere. Some days I am still angry, at her, at my dad, at me, at the doctors, it doesn't matter, I am just angry. I get into my feelings sometimes, and don't get out of my Pyjamas, and watch old I Love Lucy reruns like I used to with her. Grief is strange. It lives in the small places no one else can see. It happens some days, when I can't even express why I feel the way I do.

There was a point where I hit rock bottom.

People don't really talk about that part of grief. They talk about being sad, about missing them, about crying. They don't talk about the anger. The exhaustion of missing someone so much that you don't really care about anything anymore. The days when getting out of bed felt like climbing a mountain. I wasn't just sad. I was lost.

The person I called for everything was gone, and I didn't know who I was supposed to be without her. I was going through the motions of life. There were days when the only people I talked to were my husband and kids, but it all seemed surface-level. I wasn't really saying anything. Days that I wouldn't leave the house, didn't want to shower, or cook. The day I stayed in the shower and cried so no one would hear me. Grief doesn't just break your heart.

Sometimes it breaks who you thought you were. But eventually, life does what it always does.

It keeps moving. And whether you are ready or not, it pulls you with it. I started laughing again, cooking again, being present again without the guilt. Not because the grief went away. But because I learned how to carry it without letting it carry me.

IT'S BEEN ALMOST eight years since I talked with my mother.

So much has happened, that I wish I could share with her. She was always my biggest cheerleader for anything I did in my life. I could call her and tell her I finally mastered a recipe that I had been struggling with and she would celebrate with me.

Literally, she would shout "WHOO HOO!!!" on the phone. I could talk to her about anything and everything. No matter the time of day or night, she would always answer the phone. Losing a parent is the moment you realize you are not a child anymore, no matter how old you are. When my mom died, I felt like the roof of my life disappeared.

The first holiday without her happened just two weeks after she passed. Christmas. My mother loved Christmas, she always made sure that it was magical when we were kids even when we got older, she kept the magic going. That first holiday wasn't too bad. I think I was still in shock that she was gone. It was the next year that was really tough.

I felt guilty about doing all the things without her there. Over the years, I have had less feelings of guilt. It's weird, you know, how it never really goes away; it changes shape. Some days it hits out of no where and I want nothing more than to stay in bed all day and shut the world out. I wish she was able to see my kids growing up, she has missed so many huge milestones with them.

I am afraid that one day I will forget what her voice sounds like. That is what scares me more than doing life without her. I wish there were times when I could reach for the phone; some days, I still do. I still have her number in my phone, I don't think I will ever erase it. It feels like I am erasing her if I do. I used to think grief was something you got through. Now I think it's something you carry with you for a lifetime. I carry it when I cook her recipes, when I watch I Love Lucy reruns, when I want to call her and can't. But I also carry her laugh, her voice, her stories. The watch.

And I think maybe that is what grief really is. Love. Love that doesn't have anywhere to go anymore. **I am no longer who I was before she died.** But I am still here. And I think she would be really proud of that. I still have that watch. The battery is dead now. It doesn't beep at 1:17 anymore.

Sometimes I think about changing the battery and hiding it somewhere, just in case she comes looking for it again. I think she would laugh at that. I think she would laugh at me crying over a stupid pink watch.

Grief is strange like that.

It doesn't live in hospitals or funerals or sympathy cards.

It lives in jewellery boxes. In old TV shows. In phone calls you can't make anymore.

Sometimes, it lives in a watch that still feels like it belongs to both of us.

17

WITH LOSS, COMES HOPE

DEANN SOLEIL

Mention of Cancer, Loss of a Loved One- Grandmother, Navigating Grief, Alcohol Use

Sometimes life hits you in unexpected ways through loss. Grief is one of those things that can either make or break you.

For me, it made me hit rock bottom.

Through support and change, you can find the hope you need to survive through some of the toughest times.

KAYLA

Have you ever been in a situation where you look around and feel like there is nothing that you can control anymore?

What about when you build relationships and have trust in others, then go through a significant loss?

That was me.

I have always been the type of person who has been strong and keeps myself together, so the world around me doesn't know when something is eating at me inside. If I say so myself, I do a pretty damn good job at it, too. Nine times out of ten, people don't realize what can be eating at me inside.

As a social worker, I always live by the idea that I should have my life together in order to help other people, but I've realized that's not always the case. There are days when I let down my walls and can relate to some of the stories others are going through.

Social workers are human, just like others we interact with. It's okay to acknowledge when we're not okay and take time for ourselves when we feel like our backs are up against a wall. Sometimes we need to take the advice that we give to other people, but it can be hard to do that, especially when loss comes into play.

Grief can cause people to go through a life change, especially if it's someone you're close to and talk to every day.

I lost my grandmother far too soon. The woman whom I talked to every day and spent a lot of time with throughout my lifespan. She was one of my rocks that I had when I was navigating challenges that I didn't know what exactly to do with them.

Going from receiving a cancer diagnosis to her being suddenly gone flipped my world completely upside down. The thoughts that would run through my mind were, "She was just fine a month ago." I had literally seen her a few days before we received the call that we would need to get to the hospital because she wouldn't make it through the day.

That call was one that changed my life for good. I made the hour-and-a-half drive to the hospital she was in, watched her body change colors, and held her hand during her last breath. That vision is one that will stick with me throughout my whole life.

That was one of the hardest days I've lived through.

I tried to keep my cool and not let others see how much it impacted me, but I couldn't do that anymore. It took so long for me to wrap my brain around the fact that I couldn't just pick up the phone to hear her voice anymore.

I hit rock bottom.

Hard.

Fast.

The kind of rock bottom where I didn't want to do anything at all. I wanted to bottle myself up in my house and not go anywhere. Alcohol became a crutch that I wasn't sure if I could move past or not. Turning to the bottles of wine felt so right. Over time, I realized that alcohol doesn't cure everything. It was just a temporary solution, as I was coping.

There were plenty of nights when I would sit on the floor of my house, bawling my eyes out because I couldn't see her anymore. The text messages and voicemails that filled my phone made me know I could never delete them. I would need to keep them around for as long as I could.

In that moment, I truly learned what grief felt like, and that I needed to process my emotions. Listening to the messages just caused more tears to fall, but I knew that it needed to happen. Hearing her voice from time to time was something that could bring joy on some of the darkest days.

I would see other people talk about losing a loved one that they were close with, but I never understood what it would feel like for me.

Yeah, I've lost some family members, but not someone whom I was able to talk to about random things on a daily basis. That relationship was so different than any of the other ones that I have ever had.

❊❊❊

The concept of hitting rock bottom might look different for everyone, depending on the situation that they are in. It can be a loss like mine, constant negative ruminating thoughts, or a shift in life. The many different experiences that people navigate make them who they are today. It shows the ways that some people can face being at rock bottom head-on, or needing to take a mini step back to figure it out.

It's so important to not judge other people when they are navigating any type of loss. This can cause them to be more triggered and not come out of the deep, dark place they may have buried themselves in.

When I would turn to the bottle to keep me going or turn to isolation, I began to realize that's not a healthy coping mechanism. Being able to connect with other people who truly care and want to see you come out of being at rock bottom is what matters the most.

If there's any time you feel like you can't pull yourself up or feel like there's nothing to look forward to anymore. It's important to lean on those who want to support you. This can be a partner, a family member, or even turning to therapy. Sometimes there is some hesitancy that may come from therapy on whether it will be a good match or not, but push through and test it out anyway.

During that time, I felt like there was nothing to look forward to because there was so much grief to process. I had looked at all the upcoming milestones that were waiting for me in life that she wouldn't be a part of. This made me feel like there was no hope until I got help.

Starting therapy was an adjustment at first, but I realized it was what's best for me. I found someone I meshed well with who helped me keep going, and I know that there's a path for me that my grandmother would be proud of. I won't lie, it took some time to really get accustomed to talking about my problems, but I quickly learned it was something I needed to do.

Grief is something that has stuck with me, and I

think about her every day. I look for the cardinals and recognize that she's still with me, even if I can't physically see her in front of me. Knowing this and leaning on the support system I have today has shown that there is hope, even when I felt like rock bottom was my only choice.

Always look for the signs around you that show your loved one is with you, because that will help you keep on going, as it did for me.

18
BLACK AND GOLD

LEE ADAM

"Derek, I'm sick and tired of going around and around like this!" Murray groaned.

"Why are you saying that like it's *my* fault?"

"I never said it was *your* fault, did I?" Murray stopped, opened his mouth, closed it again, then continued pacing, tracing the same route he had done countless times before.

"Well, to be honest, Mur, I don't see what the big problem is." Derek fell in line, following close behind. "I mean, we're safe, warm, and have three square meals a day. What more could you want?"

"Freedom." Murray stopped in his tracks and whipped round, forcing Derek to slam to a halt. "I want excitement and adventure," Murray continued, "I want to break out of this jail cell, see the ocean and swim with sharks."

Swim with sharks?" Derek snapped. "Are you listening to yourself?"

"This isn't living, Der, it's barely even surviving. We're prisoners, held against our will without due process or possibility of parole. I need more."

For the longest moment, Derek stared back at his friend, opening and closing his mouth but saying nothing. Then he screamed, "YOU. ARE. A. FISH! What do you mean you wanna swim with sharks? You have a death wish or something?" He swam to the glass, pointing his fin. "You've been watching too much of that glowing thing with the little people in it."

"Eh, it's called a picture box, Der." Murray condescended, already bored with the rant.

"I don't care what it's called, *Mur,*" Derek snapped back. "It's a lot of crap, and it's filled your head with stupid ideas again. Remember last week? You were convinced you were a dinosaur because of that thing."

"No, I don't remember." Murray turned and swam away, petulant and defiant.

"Or the time the picture box convinced you that there had been a murder and you were the only one who could find the killer?"

"You explain what happened to Sponge Bob then," Murray snapped, pointing an angry fin. "He stood next to that castle for as long as I can remember, then one day they cleaned out the bowl and he's gone. What happened to him, Der? Huh? He was my friend, I can't just let that go."

"He wasn't your friend, Mur. He never said one word to you the entire time he was here."

Murray opened his mouth to reply, but before he could, the room door swung open. Two big people walked in, stopping right beside the table where the fishbowl sat. Murray and Derek instantly recognised the smaller person with the yellow hair. She was the feeder. They liked her, but neither of them recognised the taller one. He had black, wiry hair and thick stubble on his chin. His face was orange, and his hands swung as he yelled.

"What d'you think's going on here, Der?"

"How the hell am I supposed to know?" Derek replied as he swam away with disinterest. "I don't speak people language, do I?"

Murray pushed his nose to the glass, his eyes widening. He watched as the black-haired man barked at the feeder, and she yelled back. Then, black hair pushed Feeder, and she stumbled back a step.

The long moment of silence was broken when Feeder whipped her hand out, connecting with black Hair's stubbled jaw. His head snapped towards the fishbowl. Just then, something plopped into the water and sank to the bottom. The two fish scurried in wild circles, kicking chunks of the small gravel and dust that lined the floor of their home.

The black-haired man stumbled and slapped his hands down on either side of the bowl, jostling it dangerously close to the edge of the table. The man stared straight down into the water. Derek ducked for cover while Murray was frozen in place.

Murray felt his mouth pumping faster and faster as it struggled to keep up with his racing gills. He looked up. At this distance, the stranger's face occupied Murray's entire field of vision. He could see the split in the man's top lip as blood trickled down, then fell into the water.

"Get out of there, Mur," Derek yelled from behind the ornamental castle at the far end of the bowl, but Murray was transfixed; paralysed with fear. Man and fish. Eyes locked. The man snarled and tongued the tooth in the corner of his mouth. All Murray could do was stare as the giant's face turned from a deep tan to an angry red.

In a burst of movement, the man spun and grabbed the Feeder by the throat. She fought back, and they both fell to the floor.

Murray fluttered back and forth in a panic. "Derek, Derek! He's hurting her. Derek, what do we do? What do we do?"

"Hide, you idiot!" Derek screamed.

In a flurry of fear, Murray scuttled around the castle and hid.

The pair hung still, save for the sucking motion of their mouths, for hours. (In actual fact, the two were there for only a couple of minutes. Fish aren't very good at estimating the passage of time.)

They both edged an eye over the castle's rooftop in time to see the stranger stand up. Murray glanced down and saw the lifeless feet of Feeder on the floor, her body hidden by the sofa. The black-haired man's eyes bulged as he stared at his hands as though noticing them for the first time. The rage in his eyes was replaced with a mixture of panic and disgust.

After another hour (again, just a few minutes, they're fish, remember), the stranger snapped back to the present and rushed out of the room. He returned as quickly as he left, pulling wipes from a pack. He crouched down and disappeared behind the couch where the body lay.

Derek and Murray crept from their hiding spot and did a fish's equivalent of tiptoeing towards the glass to get a better look. Closer and closer. Inch by inch. Nothing. Not a sound. They both held their breath, straining to hear even the slightest sound.

The stranger exploded from his crouched position, and both fish scampered back to their hiding spot. Slowly, Murray bobbed his head up, sneaking a glance. He watched as the man took another tissue from the pack and started wiping the table, door handles, and other seemingly random things around the room.

Evolutionarily speaking, the life of a goldfish is very perilous. The lakes and rivers that make up its natural habitat are teeming with predators such as heron, pike, and pretty much anything larger than the fish itself. As such, the evolutionary path of the Carassius auratus (not one of nature's proudest achievements) means the fish has a naturally high anxiety level. Ironically, being in constant fear for its life is exactly what has kept the species going for centuries.

This means that your average household goldfish is intimately familiar with the concept of panic. Fear looked and felt pretty much the same in almost every animal on the planet. Murray and Derek could see that the stranger standing over the lifeless body of their feeder was, indeed, in a panic.

The man then bolted for the door, leaving it open in his wake.

The fish were alone.

WEEKS LATER, (two days to you and I), a school of strange-looking figures with blue hands and covered head to toe in white, flooded the room.

"Der, look," Murray shouted in a whisper.

"Why are you whispering? It's not like they can hear you." Derek chided as he sidled up to Murray. They both looked on as the creatures bustled back and forth putting things into small bags. Bright flashes of light burst from small black boxes that they held to their eyes.

Derek fluttered for the safety of the castle while

Murray looked on in stunned amazement. "You'd die in the wild," Derek said.

"Huh?" Murray turned side on, keeping one eye on the action and the other on his friend. "What are you talking about?"

"You," Derek snapped. "You have no fear. You should be hiding back here with me, not trying to get closer to those… those things. Swim with sharks? You'd last three seconds out there on your own." Derek swept a fin towards the great wide beyond.

"I think they're here to help," Murray said, nodding towards the blue-handed creatures.

"How could you possibly know that?"

"I think I've seen animals like this before. They live in the picture box."

After two days of bustle, the white creatures packed up and left (Yup, you guessed it,the crime scene techs were in and out in just over an hour) and in walked two men. The taller, heavier one looked to be around 800 years old (fish are as good at estimating ages as they are at telling time), while the smaller man was a hundred years younger.

The octo-centurian hovered over the body while the other man floated around the room. He paced back and forth, scanning his eyes this way and that, then made his way to the fish tank.

"Hey, I think I know that guy," Murray called

back to the still-hiding Derek, "I think I've seen him in the picture box."

"What?" Derek said, peaking out from his sanctuary.

"Yeah, I've seen his face before."

"You can't have. The things in the picture box are tiny."

"No, I'm sure it's him. He was with that woman, fighting that thing, you remember?" Murray was getting animated now. Excited to see a picture box creature in real life. Derek plucked up his courage, sidled up beside Murray and glared up.

The man leaned close and tapped the glass of the bowl. His black hair matched his tanned complexion. Just then, the picture box man grinned, exposing the chipped tooth at the corner of his mouth. He winced and touched the fresh split on his lip.

If it were possible for fish to gasp, Murray would have gasped the biggest gasp a fish could.

"You okay, Mur?" Derek asked as Murray's eyes grew wide.

Now, I don't know how up-to-date you are on your marine biology, but in relation to the size of a goldfish's body, its eyes are relatively huge. So, for Derek to watch his friends' eyes grow even larger was both impressive and terrifying.

"It's… it's…" Murray stammered, then stared off into the distance, opening and closing his mouth.

"What?" Derek said.

"It's him, Der. It's the guy who hurt the feeder." Snapping from his daze, Murray focused on Derek. "We've got to do something." He said, his tone severe.

Now it was Derek's eyes that bulged to impressively terrifying proportions. "What do you mean by do something? What can we do? We have no arms, and don't speak people!"

"I don't know, but we have to do something." Murray's anxiety was in overdrive now, swimming in tight circles, his gills working overtime, beginning to hyperventilate. (Stop right there! Before you go adding another strange entry into your internet search history, I checked, and yes, fish *can* hyperventilate. You're welcome.)

"What do we do? What do we do? What do we do?" The words rushed from Murray's mouth, gaining speed with each repetition. With one eye, Derek watched Murray spiral into hysteria, while the other eye was glued to the killer with the chipped tooth.

The black-haired murderer rejoined his 800-year-old partner at the centre of the room. The two men talked and even laughed. The older man toured the room just like the black-haired man had done earlier, before stopping and leaning his bulk against the table where the fishbowl sat. The water sloshed back and forth, edging the bowl closer to where the man sat. The fish were now eight miles (six inches. Add depth perception to the list of things that fish know nothing about.) from where the detective sat.

"What do we do?" Murray continued, repeating it over and over like a record jumping.

"Wait a minute," Derek said, but Murray didn't hear and went on repeating his question. "Oh, shut up, will you? I'm trying to think, but I can't concentrate with you yammering on like that." His forceful tone stopped Murray dead in his tracks.

Derek eyed the policeman's back, then spun to face the empty space behind him. He turned, regarding the man again, then looked down towards the tabletop. He swam to the centre of the bowl.

"Der, what are you doing?" The panic had left Murray's tone and was replaced with one of confusion.

Derek rushed to the glass, stopped, then swam back to the centre.

"Der? Are you okay?" Murray said, sounding more frightened this time.

Derek swam to the glass again, stopped, then backed up the entire length of the fishbowl this time..

"Der, please don't tell me you're thinking about –" but before Murray could finish, Derek exploded from his position and swam for the glass with everything he had. At the last minute, he pulled up and hurtled himself out of the water, hitting the policeman on the back.

"DEREK!" Murray descended into full panic mode. He swam in wild concentric circles, then sped along the floor, kicking up loose stones as he went. The water became a whirlpool of gravel and despair.

"What the hell?" The old detective said as he turned to see a goldfish flapping on the table, gasping for a breath that wouldn't come. The animal flopped like a… well, like a fish out of water. "How did you get there?" the old man said, scooping Derek up and holding him flat in his palm. "You have a death wish or something?" He lowered the fish back into the bowl. "There you go, little fella. Wait a minute." The detective swished his hand in the water, then reached to the bottom, picked something out, and turned to his partner.

Murray rushed to the edge of the bowl, pressing his nose against the glass. Now, if a goldfish could understand English, this is what Murray would have heard:

"What have you got there, Melville?" The black-haired man asked.

"It looks like a gold tooth cap. Don't see many of those these days. In fact, Herman, you're the only person I've ever seen with one." Melville inspected the cap closely. "I wonder how it ended up in the fishbowl?"

Herman shifted his weight from one foot to the

next. "Eh, no idea. Maybe the vic dropped it in there or something." He offered. "It's probably nothing. I'll bag it anyway, give it to me." He said, holding out an empty evidence bag.

"Say, what happened to your gold cap?" Sherman asked, eyeing his partner with suspicion. "You had it yesterday."

"Eh, yeah, I, eh, it's with the dentist. It needed to be cleaned. Professionally, I mean." Sherman shifted again.

It was then that Murray called out to Derek, "Hey Der, come see this. I think you did it." But there was no reply. "Der? You hear me? I think you –" Murray turned to see Derek flat on the gravel. "DEREK!" Murray dashed to his side. "Stay with me, Der." Murray nudged at him with his nose, but Derek didn't move. "Oh, I know I said I wanted adventure, but I was wrong. Please, Der. You're all I've got. You can't leave me."

Murray could not afford the energy to panic. He focused all his strength on Derek's still body as though he could bring his friend back to life by sheer force of will. "Stay with me!" He pleaded, "I swear I won't mention swimming with sharks ever again if you just wake up!"

Just then, a clattering noise in the room snapped Murray's attention. He spun around to see the two men grappling. The Sherman had Melville in a headlock. The two men stumbled back and forth, crashing into chairs and lamps.

Melville hooked an arm between Sherman's legs and hoisted the man in the air. They both fell backwards and crashed through the picture box.

Both men lay still.

"Come on, get up," Murray willed. "You can't let him get away with killing Feeder and Derek!"

After a week, Melville stirred. Groaning, he pushed himself to his feet and fished a black box from his pocket. The box crackled, "Dispatch, this is Melville. Send an ambulance and an armed unit to my location. Suspect is unconscious but breathing."

"YES!" Murray yelled. "You did it, Der. You caught him. You sacrificed yourself to catch a murderer." Sadness caught in his throat. "I'm such an idiot. I wanted an adventure so badly. I was so busy wanting something better that I didn't see I had everything I needed right here. I'm sorry, Der. It should've been me. I'd give anything to have you back. I'd swap places with you if I could." Murray watched as Sherman was handcuffed and carried out of the room.

Murray floated in silence, his mouth opening and closing.

He was alone.

"Maybe a little adventure isn't such a bad thing." Derek groaned.

"DEREK!" Murray cheered and bolted to Derek's side.

"Just stop talking about swimming in the ocean, and I'll call us even." Derek laughed

"You're... I mean, I thought you were..." At that moment, Murray was simultaneously angry and thankful that he had no tear ducts.

"I know, mate. I'm glad I'm not fish food, too." Derek smiled. "So, who's going to feed us now?"

"Oh yeah, I never thought of that," Murray said.

"Looks like we're gonna die after all."

"At least we'll do it together." Murray helped Derek up.

"Right, lads, let's get you somewhere safe," Sherman said, lifting the bowl from the table. "The station could use a mascot, and what better one than a pair of crime-fighting fish."

19

RISKY BEHAVIOR

K.M. AVERY

Weed smoking

Alcohol use

Talks of abuse

Mention of drugs (pills)

Sexual content

Sometimes you can let your trauma and pain control you to make poor decisions.

That's what I did.

But not anymore.

CHAPTER 1- PINKY

Today is my favorite day of the year, Halloween. I couldn't be more nervous and excited for what the day is going to bring. I run up the stairs of the health food store I'm managing, my rainbow tutu flopping with each step.

The little doorbell chimes, and my regular customer, Billy, comes striding in with a hat on and his normal swagger. He reminds me of my grandpa, and ever since I started working here a couple of years back, he looks out for me like I'm his granddaughter.

"Hey, Pinky! I brought you a treat."

He has been calling me Pinky since I dyed my bleached blonde locks hot pink a couple of months back. He fishes in his pocket, pulling out a family-sized chocolate bar.

"Happy Halloween, are you closing up alone?"

"Yeah, I sent the other girl home. It's too quiet for the two of us, plus I only have half an hour left."

He puts down the candy bar onto the counter and steals a piece of spinach out of the produce case, tossing it into his mouth.

"Alright, Pinky, time for me to get home before I turn into a pumpkin. Be safe!" He heads for the front door with a big smile on his face.

He didn't even buy anything…

"Thanks for the chocolate, you're the best! Happy Halloween!"

Billy leaves out the door as my cellphone chimes on the counter next to my register.

Ken: I can't wait to see you. I will pick you up at seven. Is it the lower or the top lot?

I contemplate if this is a smart idea for about the hundredth time since this opportunity presented itself about a week ago.

Me: Same! Lower lot, see you then!

I slam my phone back down onto the counter, trying to convince myself that I'm a big girl and I can do whatever I want. Sure, is meeting some random guy my ex-boyfriend introduced me to for a casual sexual hook up on Halloween for the first time a stupid fucking idea? Hell yeah, it is, but I need this release. Plus, Ken seems nice from what I can tell. Riff says the dude is a good man, and he will be there with me. Ultimately, that's why I even agreed to this cockamamie proposition.

Riff texted me, telling me he had a friend he lived with who was looking for a submissive girl to sleep with for a special Halloween treat this year. At first, I told Riff to go fuck himself, that there was no way in hell I would meet up with some random dude and fuck him.

After about a day of texting back and forth with Riff, he had convinced me that nothing bad would happen and I would be safe, so I agreed to let him share my number so I could get to know Ken more. Ken and I have been talking on and off every day since. Normally, about my work or his kids, but he seems to be a sweet man.

Now, six days later, I'm having him pick me up from my job and take me back to his place for one night of fun.

Hopefully this isn't my last Halloween…

The last half hour of the store being open flies by, in no time, as I am doing the closing procedures I have memorized by heart. This place has become like my second home, and I have given it my all and then some since I started here. This ultimately led me to receiving this manager's position.

Honestly, I would do pretty much anything to make more money so I can get away from this fucking town where I still have to see my childhood rapist walking free. That walking scum of the earth manages to find me at every one of my jobs, causing me to quit, until here, which is why I love being at this job.

Working my way up the food chain here, stashing money away has been my top priority since I left my ex-fiance nearly a year and a half ago.

Once I close up the store and lock the doors, I text my friend.

Me: I'm leaving now. If you don't hear from me by midnight, call me. Code word fluffy.

Star: I swear if I don't hear from you by midnight, I'm tracking your phone.

CHAPTER 2- PINKY

Ken waits for me as I lock the bottom door and set the alarm code. My heart pounds as his truck door pops open.

"Hey, beautiful, get in."

I climb into Ken's truck with my backpack over my shoulder and my water bottle clenched under my armpit. The instant my door shuts and his truck roars to life, I regret my actions, but it's too late to back out now.

I can't help but take note of his short blond hair, blue eyes, and muscles bulging from his flannel arms. I knew he said he did manual labor for a living, but god damn!

He's out of my league. I'm nearly 180 pounds and 5'2", short and chubby, those are not normally things that attract a man like him.

"Thanks for picking me up."

I hate driving and have bad car anxiety, so getting a ride was vital to making this work. Star was pissed. I'm not going to have an escape plan if I need it. Thinking back now, leaving my car here at work is probably a really fucking stupid idea.

"No problem, babygirl. I like your little skirt."

His calloused hand lands on my bare thigh, sending a chill down my spine. My mouth goes dry as I watch him steer the truck using his knee, so he can use his other hand to light a cigarette he has stuffed in between his lips.

"Um… thank you."

I try to watch the roads we are taking, but it's already getting dark, and I'm struggling to make out landmarks and road names as we descend into the mountainside. The only thing I can take note of is how we passed my ex-fiancé's brother's road where he lives, because we went there nearly every weekend.

Not even twenty minutes later, we are pulling into a steep driveway, coming to a stop next to a giant pile of wood that's in various stages of being cut up for firewood. He must heat his house with it.

"Come on, I promise we don't bite."

He winks at me, taking my bag off the floorboard, then closes his door.

Then I see *him*. Riff, standing on the porch with his goofy ass smile, helping my worries slip away.

We make it into his house, regret taking root in my pores. His giant beast of a dog comes trotting over and sniffs me, then sits at my feet. Of course, I pet the drooling beast and then examine the room. Ken's house is a dingy mess and clearly hasn't been unkempt with repairs or deep cleaning in a long ass time.

I want to scream, to demand he take me back to my car right now, but I don't because part of me doesn't give a shit as long as I get laid by this husky older man.

Since when did I lower myself to such standards to just feel needed and show some affection?

CHAPTER 3- PINKY

"Would you like a seltzer? I have the kind you said you like." Ken goes over to his fridge, pulling the door open to reveal an icebox full of just alcohol and condiments.

He hands me a raspberry hard seltzer and a beer for himself.

"Thank you."

"Of course, do you want to smoke?"

I told him over text that smoking weed helps get me in the mood, plus it soothes my nerves. As I glance around the living room and kitchen of his house, I can't help but wonder if I can trust the weed he has.

My dad may not be the most educated man, but he has taught me some things. One of them is don't trust weed that you don't know where it came from. Coming from a long-time pot head, I always listen to that warning.

"I brought my own, but I'm more than willing to share."

I spot my bag sitting on his cluttered kitchen island next to a stack of old pizza boxes. My feet stick to the floor as I make my way over, opening up my bag. His dog goes scampering off towards the living room.

Riff comes to my side and watches me pull out a little jar with my weed in it, plus my glass bowl that's in a soft case, so it doesn't break in my bag. My eyes go wide as I spot Ken pulling out a translucent yellow pill bottle with large white pills in it from his kitchen cabinet.

He pops the cap off and pulls two out, "Do you want one?"

Is this man really offering me some type of pill with alcohol and weed? How fucked up does he need to be to fuck me? How fucked up should I be to let him?

"No thanks, I don't do pills."

My tone lathered in disgust, due to the fact that pill addiction runs in my family, and I have watched both my parents struggle with it daily. I was addicted to ADHD medication at one point in college. It helped keep me up for days and helped me stay focused to be a straight-A student, but I hit rock bottom and nearly died.

So, that shit isn't happening again!

The three of us gather around the island and pass my bowl back and forth, but Riff doesn't smoke due to being on parole. After about thirty minutes of small talk, Riff removes himself, going off into his room past the kitchen.

"Let's go up to my room."

Ken takes my second drink and his fourth, leading me up the dark staircase behind us. My heart pounds in my ears with each step I take as I get closer to the top of the stairs.

I shouldn't do this! How can I be so stupid?

My thoughts consume me as I follow him to the left. He leads me into a barely lit room stuffed with clothes, shoes, and god knows what else. I feel claustrophobic as he climbs over the bare mattress onto the other side of the room after putting our drinks on his nightstand. The smell of cigarettes and weed permeates the air and probably all the thousands of fabrics in the room.

"Can you help me make the bed real quick?"

This can't be happening? The asshole couldn't even make the bed first?

My eyes nearly pop out of my head as he pulls out a machete from under the mattress.

"I can't keep it anywhere else due to Riff being on parole. Don't worry, it's fine."

Did he really just tell me it's fine that he sleeps with a machete under his fucking bed?

Then I think back to how the last time I was at my parents' house, my dad showed me nearly the same thing. Maybe it's just a stupid redneck thing? I let it go and tried not to think about it.

Against my better judgment, I help him make his bed, then climb right into it like a complete idiot.

I should run, should get away before this goes any farther!

But he grabs my chin and kisses me, that's all it takes for me to turn into a puddle.

Now I'm screwed!

CHAPTER 4- PINKY

The next morning, I wake up in a groggy panic, not knowing where I am. After a couple deep breaths, I think back to last night. Hazy flashes come through my mind. I see him behind me with his hand pressed to my throat as he fucked me while I watched through his wall and ceiling of mirrors. I later realized it was actually his closet. Then another as he lies on top of me, pumping into me with all his strength.

My pussy aches, but I have to pee, so I search the nightstand for my glasses before making my way out of the bed, without waking him. I have to wander down a small hallway past the staircase opening until I find a bathroom.

My feet stop dead in their tracks when I spot myself in the grimy bathroom mirror. My throat is bruised, and clear fingerprints are already turning a shade of purple. What catches me the most is the sheer amount of fingerprints and bite marks I have on my chest and thighs. I don't remember how or when they got there.

I couldn't have been that fucked up last night to black out and not remember most of what clearly was some of the roughest sex of my life…

My bladder aches, so I pull myself away from the mirror to relieve myself. I try to think back on every movement I made last night, but it's foggy like I can't quite get a clear, full picture.

I glance in the mirror again, taking a better look at myself. That's when I spotted the extreme dark circles under my eyes.

What the fuck happened last night?

When I return to the room, Ken is gone, but I spot my cell phone out on top of a pile of clothes. I climb onto the bed and over it to retrieve my cell. A conversation from Star is open.

My eyes skim it, but I don't remember sending her texts.

Star-R u okay? Do you need me to come get u?

Me- No, I'm good. I'm going to bed. Night!

Then I see the unopened texts from her.

Star- R u sure?

Star- Fine, good night, see you tomorrow!

Did I really text her that? It doesn't even sound like me.

"Good morning, babygirl. Here's water, coffee is downstairs," Ken says from over my shoulder.

I need to get the fuck away from here! Like right fucking now!

CHAPTER 5- PINKY

I think back to that night often, one where I willingly put myself in harm's way when I shouldn't have. I could have been kidnapped, murdered, all for the wrong reasons.

I know parts of what happened that Halloween night are not my fault, but some of it is. I should have never gone, for fucks sake, I should have never agreed to even give Ken my number, but I did. Even better yet, I should have never trusted an ex-boyfriend, let alone one who was on parole.

That was over ten years ago. A time when I made rash decisions that put my life at risk, all for the thrill and the companionship. That me was broken, one where her fiancé had broken her heart, and she searched in all the wrong places to replace that love and connection. I was on a path that was leading to one of two things: spiral into dismay and chaos, or death.

In my life, I had to deal with trauma from such a young age, health issues, and learning disabilities. With that came poor judgment and reckless behavior when I was tired of being the good girl. I had to be the good girl, the one who served her community, worked multiple jobs, took care of her dysfunctional family, all while getting three associate's degrees. I found ways to act out and seek attention.

When I was at my most reckless time of my life, I would hang out with the wrong people, meet guys off dating apps for hook-ups, and even go away with strangers for the weekend. There were even times I was reckless with my own life in other ways. I would eat my emotions to the point of severe sickness, and dealt with addictions like alcohol and pills. I swore I would never do that, but I did. At one of the lowest points in my life, I would self-harm and not care about my own well-being.

That's not me anymore. I'm stronger, healed in some ways, and have learned to not be self-destructive when I'm bored or scared. I also no longer let my abuse control me or live rent-free in my head.

I find the best way for me to not default to that recklessness is reading and writing. I get lost in all things book-related. Reading, reviewing, writing, and shopping for books has become my outlet. It grounds me, plus writing helps me see different things through different perspectives.

Reading has saved my life, given me a new perspective, and an outlook on life that I never thought was possible. Two books in particular helped me change my life in a completely different way. I read two health books and adopted a new lifestyle, which has not only helped me overcome medical issues, but also my husband. We owe our lives to books, and none of that would've happened if I hadn't picked up reading again.

I have grown and overcome the choices I made back then because, believe me, that wasn't the only sketchy situation I got myself into over the years.

Now I'm a bookstagrammer-turned-author who lives out her dreams daily doing what she loves. I have a life I'm proud of that's full of love and compassion.

I don't regret my choices because they have built me into who I am now, and I'm proud of who I'm becoming…but there is always room for growth.

Regardless of what happens in life, remember you are strong and can overcome any challenge or obstacle you're faced with…even if that obstacle is yourself.

20
DOWN AND OUT

K. D. LAVENDER

CHAPTER ONE

The beginning of the end

Johnathon

I sit and listen to the rain as it batters the windows at the front of the house. Thunder rumbles so loudly I can feel the vibrations through my body even inside the house. A flash of lightning illuminates the room for a split second before it goes dark again. I sit here in my chair lit by the dim glow of the open fireplace, on the table in front of me sits a full bottle of scotch and a packet of tablets. I tried to drown the memories before they broke me completely. I failed.

I think back to that night when it all happened and how life turned out the way it did. I wish it was all a dream and I could just wake up and everything be back how it was, but life doesn't work that way. Now I'm sitting here at the lowest point of my life only seeing one way out.

Six months, six long months. That's how long it had been since the car accident that had taken everything from me. The images haunted my dreams as well as every waking moment. Months of therapy had done nothing to help if anything sitting and talking about that night made things worse. I had relived it over and over in the therapist's office until I couldn't take it any longer and decided to stop going back there.

I crack open the seal on the scotch and pour a glass, the sound of liquid splashing into the glass brings me a strange sense of comfort for some reason. I pick up the glass and take a sip, it burns my throat and I wince as I swallow but I enjoy it. Seeing as this is my last night here I might as well do something I enjoy.

The memories of that night run wildly around my head as I drink, I hope that I can be at peace after this. I take another sip of the scotch and swallow, the burn causing me to wince once more. I try sifting through the memories still trying to find out what went wrong. Maybe the answer isn't there, maybe it was all my fault but even the tiniest shred of hope would give me a reason to keep going. The only choice is to relive the pain one last time as I sink back into the chair and begin reliving that night in my head.

CHAPTER TWO

That night

Jonathon

I'm driving down the road in the dark. The fog has set in making it difficult to see even with fog lights on. My wife sits in the passenger seat singing along to a country song, she loves her country music. My child is in the back seat bobbing away in his car seat. He just loves music, anything with a good rhythm and he dances away. The mood in the car is full of laughter and high spirits as we drive away from the in-laws house and down the dark back country roads.

I've done this drive a thousand times and I'm over confident that I know the roads well. Little do I know this will be my downfall later on. I join in singing along to the song, it's when it rains it pours by Luke Combs. It's so upbeat that I can't help but dance around a little bit in the driver's seat. I feel the car drift a little as I dance around so I ease up and get back on the right side of the road.

I keep driving through the thick fog at the speed limit thinking I know the roads better than anyone else. The twists and turns on the roads make the car lurch and lean around the corners causing my hands to grip the steering wheel tighter. The fog gets thicker and thicker as I drive but still I don't slow down, my overconfidence in my driving skills is getting the better of me.

As I drive around a corner dangerously close to the white lines in the middle of the road I'm met with headlights dangerously close to my car causing me to swerve and brake hard. I pull over onto the side of the road and turn the engine off as I start to check on everyone.

"Are you ok?" I ask my wife who's sitting there breathing heavily.

She nods her head and starts taking deep breaths to calm herself down. I turn my attention to my child in the back seat. He's sitting there crying and screaming as I try my best to console him from my seat, my own heart is pounding in my chest as I do. My wife removes her seatbelt and turns around reaching over to him trying her best to comfort him and stop him crying.

That's when I see bright headlights from a HGV barreling towards us. The driver can't see us because of the fog and the fact that with the engine off there's no lights to show him we are there. I shout to my wife a second before it hits us, sending the car barreling forward and rolling onto its roof through the hedge at the roadside. It seems like an eternity that we are rolling around, I reach for my wife as she's thrown around like a ragdoll.

A few seconds later the car collides with a tree and I watch helplessly as my wife is thrown from the car. I try to undo my seatbelt to get to my child in the back. He's not moving but appears to be breathing. His little chest is rising and falling but I'm unable to get my belt off. I hear a voice outside the car and I look around trying to get my bearings.

"THE BACK SEAT PLEASE MY SON IS THERE HELP HIM"I shout as tears stream down my face now panic has set in.

I hear the door being pulled at before I hear it giving way. I'm dizzy as I hear a voice from the back seat telling me he's alive but I can't respond, I'm in a daze. The voice from the back seat is trying to keep me calm and reassure me that it's going to be fine, they've called the emergency services. What feels like a lifetime passes before I see flashing lights approaching and I black out.

When I wake up it's the following morning. I look around trying to figure out where I am before I realise I'm in the hospital. As I look around I see my father in-law asleep in the chair next to me. I call his name hoping he wakes up.

"Brian... Brian wake up" I call, causing him to stir and open his eyes.

"Johnathon don't move I'll get a nurse" he says before running out to the nurses station.

My head is pounding as I lie there in the bed struggling to remember what happened. Suddenly a full team of nurses and doctors come flooding into the room and begin performing various checks on me. All I can think about is where my wife and child are right now. I need to know if they're ok. After a few minutes everyone but brian has left the room.

"Where's Melissa? Where's Thomas?" I ask weakly.

"Son Melissa didn't make it; she was pronounced dead at the scene of the accident." He says as tears form in his eyes.

"What about Thomas? Please tell me he's ok" I say as I begin crying myself.

"Thomas is alive but he's in a coma. They don't know if he's going to wake up" Brian says as he reaches for my hand.

Tears are running down my face as I cry for the loss of my wife and the potential loss of my son.

CHAPTER THREE

Johnathon

I spent the next six months doing daily visits to sit with Thomas hoping he might wake up but every day is the same. It's just me talking to him as he lays there unconscious in the hospital hooked up to machines. He's just four years old. He should have been playing with toys and having the time of his life, instead each day is one step closer to him never being around again.

Now I'm sitting here in the dark making the choice to take my own life because it's clear that I caused that accident. If I hadn't turned the engine off maybe we would have been seen, or if I had just controlled myself and not been so confident we would never have had the near miss.

For months I was told to hold onto the hope that he would wake up, but each day eroded that tiny bit of hope more. I didn't have anything left to hope for. The statistics all showed that he wasn't going to wake up. I had nothing left to live for. As I sit there in the chair slowly emptying the pills into my hand my phone lights up on the table. It's Brian calling. I ignore it. I don't want to hear another lecture about holding out for my son. There's nothing left in me.

The phone lights up again and Brian's name shows on the screen again. Once again I ignore it and let it go to voicemail, this time he leaves one as it shows up on my screen. The phone lights up one more time but this time it's the hospital. I pick it up bracing myself for the worst news of my life.

"Hello" I say as I answer it and a young woman on the other end responds.

"Is this Jonathon Smith?" she asks.

"Speaking I assume this isn't good news" I say, my voice is low and clearly not caring anymore.

"No Mr Smith quite the opposite, Thomas has woken up" she replies.

I drop the phone and the handful of tablets at the same time, I can't believe what I just heard. The voice on the other end of the phone is calling my name still as I sit there in disbelief. Everything I'd been told by Brian was true to hold onto hope and now my hope was renewed by a single sentence. I thought everything was gone that there was nothing left to live for but now I had hope and a reason to go on. I reach down and pick up the phone.

"I'm on my way in now, tell him daddy is coming" I say and I hang up the phone.

21

SEALED IN THE DARKNESS

A PROLOGUE

SB STRICKLAND

For those of you at rock bottom. Know that you are there now, but the only way to go is up. Find your Embers in the Darkness and shine brighter than ever before.

A SPECIAL THANKS to all my Embers; without you I wouldn't be able to shine.

ELTERANA, the kingdom of Man

What is life without death? What is love, if not war? I, Princess Astra of House Elterana, had never really listened to these questions; the old scholars that followed Father around like flies would mutter. Oh, how I should have listened to them. To Father, to the masters of healing, to the older servants, all of them. I should have listened.

Now I spend my days chained to the dungeon walls of my own castle. Thinking over my own answers to these questions. Alone. Either they captured my father, King Tyrion, or they beheaded him like a common thief. All my people enslaved or dead. My father's soldiers, all captured or dead. All because of Aethon. When I had first met him, it had been in the forest surrounding my home, the Kingdom of Elterana. I was returning from the annual peace summit when attackers ambushed the royal progress. The commoner was unusually rare for the kingdom, a Fae.

But Aethon had shown up wearing the clothes of a commoner, mere rags of grey and his hood. He had saved myself and my ladies-in-waiting from danger, and lost his hood. His features, strong. Hair a rugged blonde, with eyes deep-set silver. His skin had a sun-kissed appearance. His actions had been heroic and even daringly brave. He had been thanked profusely, and as a token of my personal appreciation, I had given him my family's firestone emeralds. They had been my mother's before me, and my mother's mothers and so on and so forth. Artisans set dark crimson stones, found during my kingdom's founding, in tarnished gold. The second king's wife received this gold as a wedding present. I had been so thankful at the time that I didn't notice - no; I ignored the signs. My father, the King of Elterana, had graciously opened our home to him. Only for him to act rigid and distant; I had made excuses, because maybe the Fae were simply shy.

Coming into the palace as if he owned it, then later inviting his own men in without consent, and again I had made excuses. They had treated everyone as if we were merely their amusement, rather than their hosts.

And as soon as he had set the trap, I, like a complete fool, fell for it. And it had been magical. The gardens that night had been alight with the moon. The smell of the flowers filled the air, and for a time I thought it had been perfect. That was until I had said yes, and my people had suffered for it, and for what reason did they kill my people? Just because they could? Because Aethon Starkrider was no mere Fae, no, his followers had called him the dark royalty. The kind that my wet nurse had told me stories about as a young girl. The kind that came and slaughtered my people for eons without a care. And for what? No one in recorded history even knows. The steps seem to echo even louder in the dark. Stinging my eyes and blinding me, the torch's bright light shone intensely. The sound of the cell door creaking open had me blinking my eyes quickly, trying to see around me. I look up to see two Fae guards dressed in black leather. Their upper armor was matte blackened leather that had a high stiffened collar that framed their neck, probably offering protection. With a diamond-quilted pattern woven in. Prominently covering their shoulders and upper body, a textured yoke. That features a woven feathered texture that gives them a sharp, menacing silhouette. A series of small toggle fasteners running down the center secures the front of their uniforms. The bottom of their tops tapers into a low V-shape in the front. Their trousers are slim but fitted, high-waisted and tailored out of thick leather. On their feet sit boots made of abolished leather, with worn slight wood and rounded toes. They stand with their blackened helmets on, keeping their features hidden. One of them stepped forward to jerk and twist my wrist free from the shackles. The sound of the heavy iron slamming into the stone floor echoed loudly, hurting my head more than anything else. My darkness has been too quiet, so the loudness makes me flinch. The other guard grabs me by the upper arm, dragging me from the cell and towards the stairs.

They literally have to drag me because my legs are just too weak, but when we reach the stairs, they do not turn left to head up to the surface of the dungeons, but right, deeper into the dungeons. I weakly try to pull myself out of their hold, but I am too weak from my prolonged confinement in the darkness. The guard on the left yanks me up roughly. "Stand up," he hissed, his voice oddly familiar. After a few minutes, they finally dragged me to the lowest level of the dungeon. A place I used to explore as a young girl when I grew bored with my teacher's lectures. As they do, we head towards a door that I do not recognize, The wood is ancient and dry. The wood held by Iron that looks as if it is as old as the castle itself.

All I truly know is that they are heading for that door and dragging me with them. Fighting is something I must do; I can not die like this. I attempt, again, to wrench my arm from their grip. Before slamming my foot into one of their feet, causing the one on my left to let go in pain. I slam my now free fist into the other's crotch with as much force as I can, making the bastard drop to his knees. I turn as the first one stands and swings my leg, nailing him in the crotch as well, sending him to his knees. Running blindly in the darkness, I take off.

Thankful that I know these dungeons from my childhood adventures. It takes a few minutes, but finally, I find it. The Castle's ancient sewers. I have barely any strength, but I slam my body into the bars. I am not sure when they were last checked because they seem to give way fairly easily, and I immediately crawl through as I hear hurried footsteps. The smell alone makes my empty stomach churn, and I have to fight not to gag at the putrid stench. I keep crawling, even when my knees are aching, my fingers are numb, and my palms sink through the feces and waste. I know I must keep going. I owe it not only to myself but to the people of Elterana, my people. When finally after what feels like an eternity, I feel a breeze. The sewer tunnel ends just outside the city, on the edge of the forest. As I crawl to its edge, I fall out. My body slamming into the mud and sewage, the cool autumn air burns my lungs in the best possible way. I know that I have to get up. Moving is necessary for me, but I cannot do it, not yet. I just continue to take deep breaths, letting the wonderful air burn my lungs. I lay as I watch the sun fade into night, and the wildlife from the forest comes alive. After countless minutes, I tiredly make my way to my feet and try to wander through the forest, stumbling over roots and beginning to wander through the forest. Stumbling over my own feet and the undergrowth. I don't know where I am going, but I know that I have to keep moving.

My foot catches on a root, sending me falling to the ground hard, my head bouncing off the ground. The palms of my hands sting, and my knees ache, but a sound of movement in the underbrush stops me in my tracks. I waited for a moment, but thankfully it was just a rabbit. I try to think of what to do now as I push myself up on shaky arms. Wandering for a time aimlessly, I can feel the weight of all that has happened fogging my mind. And before I know it, a full day has passed. The only thought I have is, what now? Now that I have lost everything, what can I possibly do? The sound of rushing water touches my ears, and I follow it until it is roaring. And when I step out of the trees, I find a beautiful waterfall. The sight is familiar, the falls of the fallen. I must have walked further than I thought. Remembering from my lessons that the waterfall lay north of the city. I sigh and step forward to at least get a much-needed drink. The water is cold against my hands, as I scrub them clean, but the water feels refreshing as I drink. I stand, and it's as if my entire world stops. Standing across the river is one of the most glorious men I have ever seen.

The first thing I notice is that he stands tall, much taller than I. His dark hair, which seemed to stop right past his collarbone, was pulled back from his tanned, structured face.

He wears a structured but multi-layered dark brown tunic with a high collar. The chest piece has dark threaded embroidery that shows what looks like ancient symbols. Textured leather segments reinforce it and form-fitted sleeves lead into integrated leather bracers that feature decorative ribbing.

His trousers are tight-fitting, ribbed charcoal trousers that tuck into his black knee-high armored leather boots, which have multiple leather straps with brass buckles locked in place. Around his waist is a wide leather waist belt that provides the structure to hold up his trousers, while thinner utility belts sit at an angle across the hips, holding daggers and his sword. Over his left shoulder is a cloak that is trimmed with dark, thickened fur.

His amber eyes meet mine across the river, and the only thing I can hear is the waterfall. A look of something and then rage passes over his face. Then I blink and he's gone, and I scramble backward. Only to slam into something hard. I turn and come face to face with the man. My breath catches because up close I can see he has flecks of gold in his eyes.

I take several steps back, and as my foot touches the icy river water, I jump forward in shock. His amber eyes never leave mine; it's as if he's looking for something. After a few minutes of silence, he walks past me, through the shallow waters of the river. Leaving me with a choice. Follow the handsome stranger and look towards the future? Or stay where I am in the depths of my fallen kingdom? After just a minute, I look to the future and take off after him. For I refuse to stay sealed in the darkness any longer.

22

ROCK BOTTOM

KC RENZEL

religious ideation

I know too well the taste of losing everything that you love.

Not in the material sense but through a spiritual lens, watching all that you know fade to dust.

Crumbling through your fingertips, survival a must, but resources are limited and help requires trust.

Sitting amongst darkness under fog of obscurity. You're told that recovery and healing is an act of maturity. I assure you that growing requires more than intention but these are the things people never want to mention.

Plants require sunlight and water, children need affection. You cannot find your new life path when you have no direction.

To be lost is not forgotten, just a point of contention unless you refuse to get better and stay in mental detention.

So sharpen your nails, dig yourself from the grave and wrangle situations, forcing them to behave.

Be brave, for its your time.

You're going to be just fine but not without

effort and sweat on your brow but tomorrow isn't promised so you have to do it now.

Perspectively speaking, rock bottom is just a strong foundation for you to build on. You never seem to really know what you've got 'til it's gone.

It takes falling from Heaven to see you've fallen for so long, but even baby birds are thrown from nests to see if their wings have grown strong.

So, the days where it feels like you're living in hell, remember you've lived on a shelf for so long that the dust feels like a fresh coat of paint.

The first step to recovery is knowing your worth and remembering your name.

23

I SHOULD HAVE STAYED HOME

A DOUBLE

racism, anxiety, fire, assault,

Scottish Glossary

Canne - Can't
Nick - Steal
Didnae - Didn't
Booted - Kicked
Fair Doos - Ok / Fair enough
Boost - Go
Here you - Hello
Fag - Cigarette
Ure ye - Are you
Ye fae - You from

A DOUBLE

"YOU BETTER SHAKE off your crappy mood, it's gonna be a great night!" My bestie Mary shouts before throwing a roll of toilet paper at me. I throw it back and continue to put on my makeup.

"I'm sorry, it just feels like one of those days. I honestly *canne* be fucked going to this party." I moan.

"Well, you better get in the mood because I'm not going without you, Missy," she sasses back.

I huff, knowing that it is a lost cause to argue. She's not prepared to stay home while our other friends are out, ergo … I'm gonna have to go out.

"Fine." I huff and finish putting on my make-up, making her smile and continue doing her hair. The more eyeshadow I put on, the more dread fills my stomach. I really wanna stay home, but I have so few friends. I don't like to disappoint the ones who put in the effort to include me. So I continue the facade of happily getting ready.

"Did you manage to *nick* any booze?" she asks.

"Naw, I *didnae*. The house hasn't been quiet, and I refuse to get caught and grounded for the summer," I say honestly.

My maw would fucking murder me if she found

me stealing her drink. Why is it always me who's asked to do it, anyway? Fuck that. We've all got parents. Someone else can take the risk. We are all fifteen going on sixteen, but I'm the only one likely to get my ass *booted* if caught. Black mums don't fucking play that bullshit.

"Did you get any from your cabinet?" I stare at her, knowing the answer already.

"Naw, I didn't. I forgot to try." She looks sheepish.

Naw, you just expected I would have gotten some.

"Oh well. We will just need to be sober until the party, won't we?"

I mean, we are already underage, and I don't wanna go. Maybe no alcohol is actually a good thing?

I pick out a nice electric blue vest top to pair with some jeans and put them on. I don't even ask for opinions on it, because I know I'm not interested in wearing a mini skirt today.

I catch my bestie watching me get dressed out of the corner of my eye, but thankfully, she says nothing. So I move on to trying to tame my relaxed afro hair into a manageable style. After the fifth or sixth tug on my roots, I give up and decide to leave it down.

I assess myself in the mirror and nod, happy with what I've achieved, but then a thought comes to mind.

"Do you think there'll be any other black people at the party?"

"Unless your brother or sister goes, it's doubtful."

I nod, knowing that would be my answer. *"Fair doos."*

Living in Scotland in the nineties, I have seen a bare minimum of other black people — unless I am related to them. I have met many Asian people and gone to school with quite a few, but they all tend to keep to themselves. So we don't mingle much.

"Right, I am good to go. If we leave now, we can get the next bus," she chirps.

Aww man. I hate the bus. So many weirdos, but how else do you get around when you don't have a car?

"Kool, let's boost."

"THIS IS TAKING FOREVER. How long until we get there?" I whine, flopping back in my chair and accidentally kick the seat in front of me for good measure.

"It's usually about fifty minutes to get to Knightswood *fae* here," she states.

I check my watch and see we have only been on the bus for twenty.

Fuck sake.

I stare out the window and watch the streets fly by below. Fruit stands and Indian clothing shops line the way below, making the journey colourful.

The longer we are on the bus, the fuller it gets, making me even more anxious. Many people stare at Mary in her over-the-top outfit, and me in my mild, polar opposite fit.

Most of them mind their business, but a loud ruckus of laughter comes from downstairs, and I immediately don't like it. I stare wide-eyed as a group of seven boys dressed in adidas tracksuits come up the stairs, look around, and then head in our direction.

"Please don't sit behind us, please don't sit behind us," I mutter and grab my friend's knee, letting her know I'm starting to panic.

She holds my hand tight but says nothing, even though she tenses up as well. They sit directly behind us.

Fuck.

"*Here you.* You got a *fag*?" One of the voices behind us asks.

We don't turn around, and we don't fucking answer.

"Oy, I'm talking to you," he snaps.

Out of nowhere, my shoulder is jostled hard,

and I lurch forward. I turn around without thinking, and am met with angry faces staring at me. My heart hammers against my chest, but I try to keep my face neutral.

"*Ure ye* deaf? Huv ye got a fag?" The ring leader speaks on their behalf.

I gulp, my mouth suddenly dry as fuck.

"Naw, I don't, sorry." I croak out.

I hear gasps behind me as I sit forward again.

"She sounds just like us, man. What the fuck. She must be making fun of us?"

"Aye, she must be taking the piss," another pipes up.

Aww crap, this is really bad.

I look out the window to see if I can recognise where we are. The need to get off the bus and bolt, followed by the feeling of wanting to vomit out of fear.

"Where *ye fae*?" Someone shoves my shoulder again.

"The Gorbals," I answer.

"Naw, where are you really fae? Black cunts aren't made in the Gorbals," they snigger, and my friend's grip on my hand increases.

"Well, that's where I'm from." I bite back angrily, sick of having to justify my heritage when I was born here, in Scotland, just like the rest of them.

Whispers pick up behind me, and I try to listen,

but I can't hear past the pounding of my heart in my ears. I hate that they are sitting behind us. I hate that I can't hear what they are saying. Waiting for their next words fills me with dread. I look at my mate, and the sympathy in her eyes tells me she's sorry I'm in this situation. *Never should have taken the bus.* Too late now, though.

A click sound behind me has me listening more intently.

Click. Click. Click.

What the fuck is that noise? A *guffaw* of laughter grates on my nerves because whatever their inside joke is, they are enjoying it.

Click. Click. Click.

The smell of burning fabric hit me. Smells like the start of a bonfire mixed with something synthetic. *I hope these idiots aren't burning the seats on the bus.* I shuffle forward, trying to put some distance between myself and the assholes.

Click. Click. Click.

The smell gets stronger, but so does a familiar smell. Hairspray. My neck suddenly feels warm, and my eyes widen in realisation. I pat my neck, and the group of guys burst into full-blown howls.

They've set the bottom of my hair on fire.

Mary and I leap from our seats and swat at the flames.

A scream bursts from my throat as I hit my neck harder, thinking my whole head is about to go up in smoke. The guys quickly get up and go running for the stairs to get off the bus. Likely realising the severity of what they've done, but giving zero fucks.

"It's out, it's out," Mary reassures me, but I continue patting my head.

The smell of singed hair deep in my nose, and I try to blow it out while wiping away my tears. I look up in time to catch one boy hovering at the top of the stairs, watching with his blue eyes full of humour.

"You should have given us a fag," he shrugs and walks downstairs as if nothing had happened.

As if he didn't almost send me to the burn unit.

Other passengers act like they are blind to what they did to me, which makes the whole thing even more sickening to me. How can grown adults watch a teenager be assaulted and sit back like nothing's going on?

I should have given him a fag, huh?

A sob breaks from my lips again.

"No. I should have stayed at home."

24

EMPTY CHAIR, BRUISED HEART_

PASTEL WREN

My tiny *arms* ***reached for*** *him, calling out his name,*
A fading whisper lingered. "You are to blame!"
An empty chair at the table, a reminder of him there,
This fucking ache inside my chest is far too much to bear.
My ***dad****, my world, my protector, suddenly is gone.*
Swallowed by the night, leaving me alone to mourn.

Ignoring me, like a ghost upon the ***breeze****.*
Leaving me reeling, my heart weighed down with unease.
Then in comes ***a*** *stranger, with his hugs so snuggly warm,*

But *in my* ***fragile*** *heart and gut, I sensed*
a *brewing storm.*
His intentions were soon very clear.
My heart ***is*** *broken and overwhelmed by*
fear.
My joy slowly diminished, taken piece by ***piece,***

MY SHINING LIGHT GREW ***DARKER*** *AND*
THE SHADOWS INCREASED.
My house was now my living hell. A
prison held me tight.

My innocence had faded, engulfed by *the night.*
My heart was now ruined and replaced with
despair.
Every day, reminders of the burdens I must
bear.
The little girl who once rejoiced from then
on was concealed.
Lost in the echoes where grief was
revealed.
Now, *to mend those wounds, wishing my*
brain would restart,
To reclaim my strength and power amid a
broken heart.
Though *the shadows linger leaving scars*
upon my ***soul,***
I will not be restrained by Sorrow's Dark
Toll.

Girls turn into teens
Teens turn into women
Forced to conform
Their voices are forbidden
Magazines shout "You're too skinny!"
Socials say "You're too fat!"
Criticised by judging side-eyes ***"She shouldn't be wearing that!"***
And yet ...
Boys will be boys
She shouldn't go out alone
If she really didn't want IT
She shouldn't have followed him home.
Why's she acting like that? She's such a dirty whore!
But look at how cool he is!
He's a slut, so funny and adored.
Beneath the headlines that scream progress,
No changes is being made.
Just another day in this world,
That a little girl is afraid.

25

HOW TO BE A BLACK SHEEP IN A WORLD THAT EATS LAMB PIE.

SILENT TREATMENT: WHEN PSY-OPS IS SERVED COLD TO EMPATHS

IVY GRAVES

conditional love, child neglect, recovering from long-term narcissistic abuse, parental bullying, undiagnosed neurodivergence, mental health neglect, lifelong suicidal ideation, no-contact, learning boundaries, healing starts when you walk away.

One of my favourite things to say as a writer is this: If you don't want to be the villain in someone's story, don't be a fucking cunt!

I want to vomit the whole time I'm writing this, just so you know.

I'm a curse-breaking shield maiden for my kids.

My parents used me as a shield to delay their karma. They are stuck in the matrix, but I escaped.

This healing journey is a long and winding labyrinth. You have to navigate it blindfolded, and no one ever tells you that the devil lives inside those closest to us. That demon Agent Smith disguises itself as the people who are supposed to love you.

No wonder people don't do it. This is hard, difficult soul-searching.

Only the strongest people survive rock bottom, because it is that liminal space where you either give up, or set the bridge you're standing on alight and forge a new path forward.

A solitary path.

A path where you put yourself first.

And those who claw their way out have the empathy to look at other people stuck in the black hole, and they throw a rope back in to save them.

That's what I hope this anthology does.

Send a rope to someone in the void of depression.

But I'm doing it because I know it's going to reach someone who needs to read it, and then not feel so alone. Maybe even help them live another day.

To know that even at rock bottom, there is a reason to get up tomorrow. Life does deliver on your dreams, but not always how you planned. Or even wanted.

Sometimes it's even better.

I feel like I am writing this for a reader who feels like they are going crazy. Unable to understand why the people who are supposed to love you leave you feeling angry, sad, hollow, lonely, exhausted, and confused.

SITTING down on Mother's Day to write about **rock bottom** for this antho as a Gen-X who was the only child, black sheep, and scapegoat … Yeah.

Fun times. No wonder I've been procrastinating THIS project.

Where do I even start?

How about rape on the beach under the age of 14? Lured there by a friend, abandoned with a grown man, and left terrified and alone as this faceless stranger molested me. Nah, that was a long time ago. Again, handy character development for my fiction.

How about religious brainwashing for most of my schooling? Nah, that's come in handy with my writing.

How about the number of adult men who touched me inappropriately, both under and over the age of 18? No, that trauma has finally started leaving my body?

Hmm, rock bottom, rock bottom.

Let me think about this now.

Maybe I could go into detail about the surrender to the pain of 24-hour labour and childbirth?

Well, from that pain I became a fierce, protective mother. That pain was worth it. Others, were not.

Like the time I asked for divorce from my ex husband. Instead of signing the papers, he repeatedely threatened to kill himself, overdosed, in and out of hospital, the whole nine yards. The tears. The psychological torture he put me through. He said, "Well, I'm going to kill myself then, and it's going to be your fault."

AND THEN WENT THROUGH WITH IT.

Because that's what rock bottom looks like when you don't claw your way out.

Or before that time, when he cyber-stalked me, breached my personal data, registered domain names in my government name, on the phone to me at my work, threatening to publish private photographs without my consent unless i went to counselling and fix our marriage. Mind you, these blackmail threats were AFTER the the time he abducted me in my own car, cool calm and collected, then when I got in, he locked the doors and sped through the streets of inner city Sydney, screaming that he would kill us both at high speed, because till him, he meant TILL DEATH DO US PART.

So, that moment in the car could have been rock bottom, but no. That wasn't anywhere near the biggest trauma I have to repair? Nah. When he stalked me for a month, calling me and making me listen to him open the pills and swallow them down. I was curled in the fetal position, begging him to tell me his location so I could send an ambulance. He'd swallowed a handful of pills again.

How about when I had to get the police to come and open the door because I just knew he was finally dead inside that door, and I didn't want to see it.

Nah, I've healed through that. A little.

No, the real sting is the pain of a thousand cuts from my parents. The decades of pain they brought upon me.

Maybe it was the fact that my parents were my first and longest-running bullies. Yep, that would probably be it.

The long-term belittling? The snarky comments? Outward displays of disgust and disapproval in all my authentic magnificence.

Nothing was ever good enough. They always directed the narrative on how I was perceived in the world. Making everyone think the wrong thing about me. Making sure all the stories they told about me were humiliating. Never showing me dignity or respecting my sovereignty. Yet demanding unquestioning respect. Crossing all my boundaries to make me look like the villain.

The daily bullying and humiliation for clearly undiagnosed neurodivergence? My sensitivity issues were dismissed and unaccommodated.

Not only the lack of access to mental health services, but the outright stigma against mental health medication and psychological therapy. Feeling isolated, triangulated, harassed, stalked, and psychologically attacked. Blackmailed, threatened, and stalked again.

Suicidal ideation.

Creativity.

I started choosing self-respect over self-sacrifice. I listened to my inner wisdom and stopped believing the lies of future promises that never eventuated.

Spiritual healing and in so growing, teaching, and providing a safe space for younger versions of me. I speak in riddles, archetypes, and symbols.

Sometimes you just know something, but can't explain how. Your higher self knows something is wrong, but you can't explain your way out of it. Narcissists love word salad. They get off on confusing you. They don't want to hear you; they want to win the argument.

I am now the middle-aged woman I would have hoped to meet when I was a child. Or fourteen. Or forty.

I'm the kind of caretaker, ally, and friend I wished would come and rescue me from a childhood so painful that I am still recovering from it as I prepare to turn fifty. I will never recover from the absense of a mother who was a soft place to fall. She never allowed me to open up to her, because when confronted, my problem was always my fault. Go away and fix it.

My children will never know the pain of isolation like that. And if I'm not proud of anything else in my life, I'm happy with knowing the truth of that last sentence.

I've done my job, I've healed. And I hope one day you can say the same thing.

Not everyone does does the hard work to level up spiritually. Not everyone has the balls to walk away from toxic dynamics like that. And even though I don't have actual testicles, I know my metaphorical balls are bigger than both my asshole parents combined. And when you realise that fact in yourself, it's time to walk away.

GROWING up on the glittering beaches of Sydney in the 80s. Sounds ideal, right? Panel vans, mullets and a wanderlust that is unrivalled. Pub music and sport galore.

Carefree, fun, active.

Where we grew up on a healthy diet of emotional and spiritual neglect, rape, and paedophilia disguised as family beach culture. Where diet culture was strong, and eating disorders were inside every closet, including mine. Once you grew tits, you were a target for being groped without consent. Wolf whistles and revoltings men getting in our space and touching us. And since our fathers weren't around to teach us, in fact, they told us to do exactly as adults tell us, we all have stories of being touched, kissed, fondled on our private areas without our consent.

Consent?

Never heard of her.

Boundaries?

Where's he from?

Suicidal ideation? *Best friends forever.*

Safe people to talk to? *Access Denied. 404. FUCK OFF TO DEAL WITH IT ALONE. COME BACK WHEN YOU'RE FIXED. CAUSE IT'S YOUR FAULT YOU'RE A FUCK HEAD ANYWAY.*

Being queer of any description was just another excuse to be dehumanized, mocked.

Treated as less than. This is why I do the things I do. This is why I teach my collective about consent, boundaries, and ways to explore the world without falling into the predator's traps. I'm here to teach young people that not everyone has the best intentions.

Snakes in the grass.

Predators in your own family. Groomers, who raise children to sit down, shut up, go to your room, wait till your father gets home, you're a brat, lose the attitude, don't back chat, eat your meal, there are starving kids in Africa.

Oh, fuck off.

Times have changed a little. Bullies are still everywhere, but they are now being called out and ostracised in real time.

Finally.

In the 70s, 80s when I grew up, Sydney was a place where bullies, xenophobes and racists all mingled together in school or in the pub, and patted each other on the back about what good blokes they all were.

Then they all went home, and now the PDF files

and survivors are testifying, so now everyone knows what happened behind closed doors. Or, in the open, as the case may be.

But for many of us who were raised in cultures where children had no boundaries, it's painful and terrifying to navigate. We're told not to listen to our bodies when they're screaming for a dirty old man/uncle/priest to get away. We're told to shut up, act pretty, kiss them, let them touch you, because they're the grown-up/god's mouthpiece/teacher/coach, so they know everything, and you know nothing.

Vile. Putrid. Toxically crippling environments, when you're a child on your own in the world. And your absent parents didn't give a shit what happened to you.

Yeah. So.

With the heady scent of board wax, ablism, full-leaded petrol, cigarettes, hairspray, and coconut oil in our nostrils, what hope did we have of growing up and having our heads screwed on properly?

The stigma attached to any kind of mental health care or support for disabled people.

So, from those lofty beginnings, rock bottom couldn't be anything but raw, brutal, lonely, and painful.

Life isn't sunshine and unicorn farts down under, despite whether that's what people think is going on from the tourist ads.

It's not. Look around you. Pedos, creeps, perverts, manosphere, and their goddamn nut job mothers enabling it all.

Holy fuck.

When are grown-ass adults going to take some accountability for how they've psychologically damaged generations of kids?

I know where it ended, that's for sure. So I'm just gonna spit straight facts.

Rock bottom ended for me the day I walked away from the two people who were my first and longest-running bullies. The day I stopped them from siphoning my light.

NO CONTACT. What a breath of spiritual fresh air. Breaking the chains. Return to sender on all those evil words spoken over my life.

It smells like sweet orange blossom, like the salt of the sea, mist of the forest, and like magic smoke wafting into your life.

And new adventures await, my friend. They are always around the corner. At fourteen, I was sure I'd be dead by 24. At 21 a doctor told me to stop having anxiety, or I'd be dead by 30.

Yeah. But here I am, approaching 50.

Life is beautiful. I am living in alignment with who I am on the inside now, and I get to share every day with the love of my life and the beautiful family we've built together. My foundations are solid, but that's not by chance. That's because I've fought tooth and nail to get here, and something happens with perimenopause. You stop trying to please people who wouldn't piss on you if you're on fire.

And I learned who was there for me in my darkest hours. Those long night's post partum, when I thought I was going insane. The pressure and the responsibility.

Because it's not always sunshine and unicorn shit, remember? Most of the time, it's Gremlins after midnight. It's puke, tears, frustration, vomit, anxiety, soul-searching, and pleading for some basic human decency. Trying to decipher how the people who raised you actually did so little to help you flourish. They clipped your wings and then gossiped behind your back. Speaking evil and ill intent over my life.

But I have a strong spiritual foundation, rooted within me, and through years of meticulous research, learning, healing, and growing. This is how I can now stand ten toes down in my beliefs and use my talents and wisdom for good. This is what makes me a High Priestess, who has been cloaked as a misfit all this time.

I'm not evil. I am duality.

Words are magic; I know this. I am a spiritual alchemist and healer.

A divinely guided and heavily protected soul who straddles the realms.

I knew this when I was born, but half my life is

missing from childhood amnesia. I am here to help other people heal, and I do this in many ways; being a wordsmith is only one way I do this.

Not like the shitstorm family I was born into. The people who chased with greed, status, and power as the carrot dangling.

I was making sure I was doing everything in my power to break that cycle.

Bettering myself so that I can go back to those I love with an explanation of why I am the way I am.

But that's too confronting. To take accountability. The ego gets very bruised. It hurts to own up to the shit you've done that hurts people.

It requires emotional intelligence and self-awareness that some people will never harness. And I gave some people almost five decades, and I decided that's long enough.

Those people can't come with you into the future. Not where you're going. Where you're going, you need a team of people who talk the talk AND walk the walk.

Begging to be treated like one of the people they dazzle with their charisma and acting skills.

Their level of insidiousness is enough to write tomes.

Tomes, I tell you! The years of neglect, silence, and not caring about my feelings. I hurt. But I was never the problem.

But I won't bore you; I'll cut to the shorthand

version of the long, boring, tear-and snot-filled years.

I'll fast forward past all the pain and torment, the coercive and dangerous relationship that I escaped (barely), to the day I blocked my birth givers and retracted my signature from a (coerced) power of attorney paperwork.

That's the day I began living for myself, and it was the first day that I felt relief of unburdening myself from their expectations. The day I could allow myself to not be afraid of them and the way they continued to bully me for being my authentic self. The day I dropped the mask was also the day I reclaimed my identity, boundaries, and stood up for what I truly believe in.

The adults whose only job was to pour love into me instead poured their hate and judgment. For decades. Bit by bit. Piece by piece. Shunned and discredited me for my creativity. Because it didn't fit into their idealized version of what art and expression should be.

We will love you as long as you fit into this preconceived notion of what we think you should be.

And when confronted with that fact, I watched the narcissistic playbook play out in real time.

With healing comes pattern recognition. Those scripts continue to play out as they have done millions of times before.

Accountability denied, flipped the script, and blamed me for doing something when I was a teen, or yet another joke where I was the punchline (again, when my frontal lobe wasn't fully developed).

Two grown-ass adults who had me so gaslit and worn down psychologically and emotionally that I didn't even know myself anymore.

Figuring out that my identity never formed properly, that there were pieces of my identity strewn up the coast of Australia.

The biological egg and sperm donors who said they didn't need therapy; they had never needed it! Yet the last time I saw them, one was throwing a toddler tantrum, literally. Sobbing and wailing, flailing and playing the victim. She cried, "You hate me!" and all I could think was, now you know how I felt all my life.

The other, the absent one, the one who traded my happiness for shiny awards and credits, was crossing all kinds of personal boundaries, squaring off with me like he was about to invite me outside and smash my face in. Mind you, he bravely waited until my husband wasn't there.

But my kids were watching on.

Yes, children.

Yeah, nice. Old man. Great example for the grand kids there. Great emotional intelligence. Self restraint.

No, I have no explaination why your grandfather is flying off the handle, starting chaos out of nothing.

All I can tell you is what I've observed closely for 48 years.

He is exactly the kind of tricky person I warn you about. The ones who wait until you're alone to threaten, coerce, and guilt you into doing soething they want you to do. But don't worry, you'll never have to see that creepy again.

We have kinder people to introduce you to.

Not like the man who gave me life, then traded my joy for his career and an attempt to impress his colleagues.

I'LL TELL YOU THIS MUCH. That man is dangerous. Volatile. Cruel. Rage-filled. Underhanded. INSIDIOUS.

ENJOYING CAUSING OTHER PEOPLE PAIN THERE, CHAMP? SEEMS SO.

Well, five decades is long enough to be TERRIFIED of your EVIL parents.

My angels, ancestors, and spirit guides got me the fuck out of there that day.

To protect my flock.

No, my sperm donor is a calculating coward. A meanie who out in public is charming, pretending he's a great guy. Shouting everyone drinks, and being the good guy, winning awards and receiving all the pats on the back. Master manipulator. Just like most bullies are. They puff up their chests, but they're just toddlers with grey hair or some douche canoe on a podcast telling women to get back in the kitchen.

Meanwhile, he needs his Mommy to make his dinner and wash his jeans for him.

Pathetic pieces of shit disguised as men and fathers.

No.

Man, Father or Mother isn't an honorific you get handed. It's a fucking badge that you earn. It's not a participation award.

Somehow, you need a registration form to own a dog, yet anyone can be out here bringing kids into the world that they punish with psychological torture — silent treatment, isolation — that they use on hardened criminals.

But I was always the child in this dynamic, and I was expected to act as the emotional punching bag.

Yeah, he's a weak-ass bully; it's common knowledge. Let's his bitch wife walk all over him, spitting their toxic venom everywhere.

But that's okay. They got what they wanted. Their united front has probably left them fighting with each other. Now, I've removed my light and my spiritual protection.

But they don't need therapy. No, they're perfect!

Cough.

Cough.

Wink.

(Why do narcs avoid therapy? cause they'll get found out, of course! The secrets will be revealed. Hard, cold truths uncovered ...yeah, therapy is hard, ya'll. Healing is hard. Looking in the mirror and taking some accountability for the part you've played in someone's pain and suffering. But therapy is worth it if it means the cycle of abuse stops here, right? Right? nah....... We don't need therapy, ya'll)

Fuck me. There is no cheating the divine order; the universal laws apply to everyone. You can avoid your tower moments, but eventually they'll come for you.

Believe the patterns, people, not the empty future promises.

Learn and educate yourself on mental health. Research the signs and symptoms of reactive abuse. Look at the patterns, listen to the dialogue running through your head that you know you'll be confronted with. You can avoid the traps.

Stop walking on eggshells.

You deserve to live with a settled nervous system.

You can heal yourself when you step away from these draining dynamics.

They never come with people like that.

It took me 48 years to figure out there was nothing wrong with me; I was just raised by assholes and had forever been trying to make them proud. That stopped.

Even wrote a whole ass book to get them to see me for who I really was. But that never happens with narcs. There's never a shortage of things to criticize.

And they will certainly never take accountability for the damage they did to you, long-term.

That incessant chipping away at identity. The snide comments. The silent treatment. The emotional maturity of an infant.

But that never happened; pleasing someone like that never happens, no matter what you do.

And the day I walked away reinforced my boundaries and broke the cycle of toxicity. sheltered my kids from a life of inner monologues that tell you that you aren't good enough.

those thoughts that make you want to kill yourself.

How is it possible that parents hate their own child with such viciousness that they look at them as some kind of demon, to bully and laugh about? The pathetic punchline of their circle of asshole friends jokes. No one asking how they can help me? No. How can I help them? How can I be their parentified child yet again?

That's the day I laid the last brick in my stable foundation of knowing who I am. The day I didn't give a fuck what they or anyone else thought of me.

You either get me, or you don't.

And they never did. But you know what? Other people do! By being authentic, you find people who love you for exactly who you are.

People who do not operate on toxic, transactional love.

For standing up for my own spiritual healing and mental health.

Rock bottom is now something that I am proud of, knowing how far life pushed me. It's shattered me many times, it's fractured me in ways you would not believe.

But even at my lowest, I've always had a good heart.

And sadly, sometimes dark empaths are the only ones who can stand up to a dark personality type and beat them at their own game.

YOU'RE **a queen on the chessboard, while those fools are out there playing checkers.**

Stand in your truth.

Ten toes down.

Trust your intuition.

Fortress up those boundaries.

Walking away from toxic relationships is when the nervous system begins to repair itself. For your angels, ancestors, spirit guides, and higher self to begin the communication process with the universe.

If you're locked in a toxic family or spousal dynamic, know you're not alone. Karma is always on your side. What are your goals? What drives you? Are you on track to fulfill your life's purpose? Who is standing in your way?

Healing begins on the other side of walking away. Learn about covert, passive-aggressive narcissists. If you are confused, have gaps in your memory, cognitive dissonance, or conflicts between people's words and actions. How do they make you feel in your body? Do you feel you're losing your mind? Numb? Alone?

You are strong. You are not the problem.

You've got this. Straighten your crown.

Your own family knew you were a chosen one before you did. They wanted to block you.

Look yourself in the mirror, own your shit, and get on with building a world that you want to live in.

Focus on yourself, pour your love back into yourself and your own found family, instead of keeping the devil afloat.

Keep transmuting all the darkness that is sent your way.

Take the swords out of our backs, put there by the ones who were supposed to be on your side.

Take those swords and build the foundations of the future on your highest timeline.

If they watched you at rock bottom, then asked why you couldn't put a mask on and entertain them.

You are Stardust. Keep sparkling, keep shining.

Your life's path is lying before you. Who are you taking into the future with you?

Cut cords.

Pour blessings back into yourself.

Embrace your Empress/Emperor energy.

Trust your gut/intuition. You have the ability, trust it. Harness it. Your psychic gifts will amplify once you step away from the energy vamps.

This is your spiritual awakening.

Don't second-guess yourself. Leap. NOW.

You've got this. Surviving constant psychic attacks. But you're rising. RAISE YOUR PSYCHIC SHIELDS.

The inhalation of magic awaits – knowing your thoughts shape your reality – this is only just beginning.

Remember to keep breathing.

Eye VII

ABOUT THE AUTHORS

ivy graves

Ivy Graves is a queer gremlin from the land down under. She is 100% brat with a dirty mind and even dirtier mouth. She writes for those with acquired erotic tastes. The BDSM lifestyle, cinema, psychology, music, and art all deeply influence her.

https://linktr.ee/ivygravesart

Willow Lewis

Willow is an advocate for mental health, suicide awareness, and helping others feel seen and heard.

ginger moonwitch

https://linktr.ee/GingerMoonwitch502

Ginger comes from the forgotten Canadian province Newfoundland. Not only is Ginger a single mother to a beautiful little girl, she is also a cat mom. She is an avid reader. Ranging from dark romance, sci-fi, fantasy and horror. Basically, as long as there is smut, Ginger will read it.

A. Twisted

A. Twisted is a Canadian author who writes intelligent, fast paced thrillers, with the occasional revenge arc, and perhaps a kiss or two thrown in there somewhere.

Marney Carroll

Marney Carroll is a poet from Western Australia. She is an ally for trans people and explores themes of loneliness, healing, and destigmatizing mental health struggles.

VIVIAN RAGE

Vivian Rage is a New Zealand based writer of feminine rage fantasy.

They are drawn to the spaces where grief, gender, and power collide. Their work explores how loss can harden into anger, and how that anger transforms into voice. They write at a desk closely guarded by their three dogs, and are currently working on their debut novel.

L.V. ELDRIDGE

I'm L. V. Eldridge, a debut fantasy author from New Zealand.

I write stories about legacy, what we carry, what we lose, and what refuses to let us fall.

My work explores surviving loss and growing from it, even when the cost is high and the path forward is uncertain.

These are stories for those who keep going, long after the light has dimmed.

L. LESTRANGE

L. Lestrange is a dark fantasy and horror author who specializes in twisted fairytales, splatterpunk, and stories where beauty and brutality collide. Her work blends unsettling worlds with chaotic characters, pulling readers into narratives that are as emotional as they are unhinged.

TIM GRAYSON

My name is Tim Grayson. I am a multi-genre author who over came the foster care system.

M. T. SOMMER

M.T. Sommer writes dark romance for readers who like their love stories complicated, intense, and a little unhinged. Her books are shaded more grey than black, with a focus on sharp edges, and even sharper humor.

When she isn't writing, she can usually be found drinking too much coffee, arguing with her pets (she's never won a round—yet), and overthinking.

Not that it's helped.

Yet.

B.A. MCCLUSKEY

I am a poet positive potato

LLIANNE OLIVO

I'm a latina author and publisher. I write dark, taboo and pitch black romance.

SYLAS SEABROOK

Sylas is a sci-fi/fantasy author of books. He has

been writing since 2022 and has recently completed the 10-book YA, neurodivergent cyberpunk fantasy series "The Rise of Tribinius Cantus".

DEANN SOLEIL

Deann Soleil is a self-published author based in Virginia who focuses on writing forbidden romances. When not writing, she is a full-time social worker who works with victims of community violence to help them overcome their traumatic experiences.

If you're looking for short, fast-paced books, then look no further.

LEE ADAM

Lee Adam is a Scottish novelist writing dark contemporary thrillers about power, violence, and the people consumed by both. His work combines the pace of modern crime fiction with character-driven storytelling rooted in betrayal, obsession, and survival.

K.M. AVERY

I'm a dark romance author and have been spending the past couple months working one many different anthologys and shared worlds for this years release. I would love to do this one because I like to give back any way I can. I'm also had a trouble up bringing and feel like I have a perfect story to tell.

S. B. STRICKLAND

S.B. Strickland is a Novelist based in the historic state of Tennessee. With her first published book, included in the Fraction Chronicles Series, she has established herself as a hopeful revolutionary voice in the literary world. S.B. Strickland's writing journey began as a teen who found a passion for writing as a hobby. Her works explore themes with deep connections and wild tales, captivating readers with fantastical twists and paths to wonder along. When not crafting wondrous worlds, you can find S.B. Strickland wrangling her two kiddos. She draws inspiration from the world around her and is a passionate homemaker. All of her books are available on Amazon. Connect with S.B. Strickland on her TikTok or follow her on Instagram and Facebook @S.B.Strickland for updates on new releases and writing insights.

KC RENZEL

K.C. Renzel is a mental health advocacy author focused on poetry and romance with darker themes and ideology. The primary goal in his writing is to spread awareness about lesser explored subjects for those without the platform to do so.

A. DOUBLE

A. Double is the queen of Scottish dark romance. Her multi-dimensional characters are relatable and darkly funny. Her books touch on hard realities of themes such as inter-racial relationships, reclaiming women's sexuality, and standing up for what you believe in.

PASTEL WREN

Pastel Wren is a poet whose writing rises from the depths of personal pain and survival. Through raw and honest verse, they explore the long shadows of abuse, addiction, and childhood trauma, transforming heartbreak into art that speaks to others who've endured silence and struggle. Each poem carries a piece of their healing, proof that even in brokenness, there is strength, beauty, and the endless will to rise.

MENTAL HEALTH RESOURCES

- How common is Postpartum? 1 in 7 women suffer from postpartum depression
- Postpartum psychosis: Extremely rare that effects 1 in 1,000 women. Postpartum psychosis requires immediate medical attention. Treatment usually includes hospitalization, psychotherapy, and medication. Please seek medical care immediately.
- Men can also struggle with postpartum depression.
- What's the difference between "The baby blues" and Postpartum depression? Baby blues go away after a few days, whereas Postpartum lasts longer and more severely. Post-partum may require medical intervention.
- Postpartum psychosis is rare, yet a very serious psychiatric condition that needs medical emergency intervention. Text HOME to 741-741 to instantly connect you to a trained crisis counselor. 24/7, FREE
- Crisis Lifeline in the U.S. has a Spanish language phone line at 1-888-628-9454.
- Postpartum depression can make you lose interest in things you once found joy in.
- Loss of appetite.
- Lack of concentration

- Lack of sleep is the most common symptom of Postpartum psychosis
- If you're struggling, you're not alone. Reach out for help, call a hotline, even if you don't feel suicidal but need to talk to someone. In the USA.
- Suicide hotline # 988
- National Maternal mental health hotline 1-833-852-6262
- Free and confidential.

www.ingramcontent.com/pod-product-compliance
Lightning Source LLC
La Vergne TN
LVHW100252210926
848480LV00003B/903
* 9 7 8 1 7 6 3 8 4 2 3 2 8 *